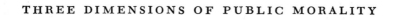

THREE DIMENSIONS OF PUBLIC MORALITY

by HERBERT W. SCHNEIDER

Indiana University Press   *Bloomington*

THREE

DIMENSIONS

OF PUBLIC

MORALITY

Acknowledgment

THE chapters that follow were presented as public lectures at Indiana University in the spring of 1954 under the auspices of the Mahlon Powell Foundation.

Preface

To Indiana University and especially to its Philosophy Department I gladly acknowledge my indebtedness for its hospitality, for the privilege of giving these lectures, and for the helpful criticism that came to me in discussion with members of the University community. Had it not been for this incitement to bring together my scattered reflections on political ethics into something resembling a system of doctrine, I would have postponed the exposition of these large themes until I could have intro-

5

duced them in their proper place in a still larger outline of general ontology. There, if they ever saw the
light, they would have been buried under the weight
of a more pretentious scheme of dimensional analysis. As it is, I have some hope that these reflections
may be read not in the context of ontology, where I
have lived with them, but in the more practical context of actual political worry and reconstruction.

Some of this doctrine goes back to my earliest
academic work, when I had the privilege of assisting
Professor John Dewey in his course on moral and
political philosophy at Columbia University. But
much of it grows out of more recent work on political theory with colleagues from other departments
of Columbia University, out of several University
seminars, and out of my present work on the theory of
human rights in connection with several UNESCO
projects. To my colleagues in these institutions, as
well as to the opportunities of working abroad in the
midst of political conflicts, I owe a much larger debt
than I can express.

Though the philosophical pattern and language
of these lectures is derived largely from the literature of political theory, I have the impression that
some of the ideas in them come directly from ob-
serving political men and ideas at work and in con-

flict. At least, I hope that this analysis of our present situation may truly emerge from contemporary facts and problems. But the primary aim of the lectures and my chief excuse for undertaking this work is the restatement of elementary truths in the science of morals, to which the tribulations of many generations and the ideas of many minds have contributed, and which I suppose to be useful and applicable in future times. The doctrinaire style of this book is due primarily to the attempt to put a whole system into a few lectures; and it fails to express my small confidence in this or any other system of assertions about human experience in general. I am trusting my fellow teachers, if they should use this book in class, to supply the missing arguments and needed amendments to the many generalizations which, without further justification, must appear as too dogmatic to impose upon students. The book is intended to start a process of critical reflection in younger minds, though for its author it is the conclusion of a long labor.

H. W. S.

Bloomington, Indiana

Contents

1
THE
DISINTEGRATION
OF
ONE
WORLD

. . . la loi divine . . . unité de Dieu en trois essences; la morale, charité; *la loi politique, c'est-à-dire,* la liberté, l'égalité, la fraternité. . . .

. . . si un avenir doit être, un avenir puissant et libre, cet avenir est loin encore, loin au delà de l'horizon visible; on n'y pourra parvenir qu'à l'aide de cette espérance chrétienne dont les ailes croissent à mesure que tout semble la trahir, espérance plus longue que le temps et plus forte que le malheur.

—CHATEAUBRIAND, Mémoires d'Outre-Tombe. *Vol. IV*

Plato told the story of how the sexes were separated by a fission of the human body, imposed on man by the jealous gods, who resented human beauty and strength and who by splitting human beings condemned them to a frantic and lifelong search for their other halves. If Plato were here, he might tell us how the devil, seeing that men were becoming reasonable, righteous, and prosperous, became jealous of their power and split their souls three ways. One third went off blindly in search of liberty, another third blindly in search of equality, and the other third preached fraternity in vain. Men thus became so self-alienated that, when the parts of the soul turned and faced each other, they failed to recognize themselves as human, for one part was warlike, another tyrannical, and a third fanatical.

It is now more than a century and a half since the French began crying, "Liberty, equality, fraternity, or death!" They did not mean, "Give us liberty or give us death!" "Give us equality or death!" "Fraternity or death!" They thought of the three as indivisible: liberty, equality, and fraternity together, they believed, would make a life worth dying for. The three ideals of the Revolutionary generation were three aspects of a single moral order. The creation of that order was not only the inspiration of the American and the French Revolutions; it continued to inspire liberal statesmanship throughout the nineteenth century. During the struggle no one questioned the essential unity of this trinity; the triple motto expressed a single faith. But in the course of time the three began to operate independently and each became inclined to go its own way. The practical divergence of the three ideals led to philosophical questioning. Are these three really inseparable?

If so, how is their unity to be conceived? Is this secular trinity, too, a mystery?

Before I attempt to explain this mystery, I should tell in outline how the three drifted apart. The drift was not apparent at first, but by this time there can be no doubt that the three-way split has reached serious proportions. The political world has now fallen apart morally to such an extent that, instead of standing together on the basis of the Enlightenment's trinitarian faith, we are divided into devotees of liberty, devotees of equality, and devotees of fraternity; and, what is worse, each of us feels within himself the tension and confusion created by the three independent ideals. I might have made my diagnosis in terms of schizophrenia, but I have chosen the extrovert language and symbolism of political geography. I shall present our "one world" as twisted into a triangular shape, its three world-headquarters or angles embodying three distinct ideals. Thus, let Washington, D.C., stand for Liberty Headquarters, Moscow for Equality Headquarters, and Rome (or rather, Vatican City) for Fraternity Headquarters. These three are embattled in a cold war of cool calculation, but each also flaunts its ideological banner hotly and passionately, imagining its particular angle to be the apex of the moral world. Admitting that there is an oversimplification in this picture, and a bit of poetic license, I still think it a true portrait of the contemporary moral crisis. For the three appear to be irreconcilable. They may be willing to "coexist" but not to co-operate. Now, how has this disintegration come over us?

Fraternity was the first of the three ideals to become detached from the trinity. Napoleon Bonaparte militarized it for the French and transformed it into national *solidarité*. In this process equality fared somewhat better than did liberty, for by his legal reforms and centralized administration Napoleon made permanent much of the destruction of feudalism and class privileges which the French Revolution had achieved. He made the "citizen" not merely a revolutionary title but a practical reality and regarded himself as the personal embodiment of the equality of all Frenchmen as citizens. Thus he soon became the symbol and champion of the revolutionary ferment throughout the world. Other peoples were inspired or provoked by him to hope for their own solidarity and equality. But as one after another of these peoples were conquered by him, he became the "little father" of the revolutionary spirit and gradually transformed this spirit into a kind of paternalism. Liberty, he thought, could be forgotten, now that equality and fraternity were reigning. Soon equality, too, yielded to imperial politics and to a new aristocracy, a new despotism. Meanwhile Fichte and his fellow-romanticists began preaching the gospel of fraternity to the German nation, realizing that for the time being liberty and equality must be postponed. Then came the Prussians, ostentatiously repudiating liberty and equality and imposing a more-than-Napoleonic fraternity on the other Germans. What equality was achieved came paternalistically —from "above" and not from "the gutter." Many of the reforms demanded by the liberals were granted by a benevolent, illiberal autocracy, and so were the social services which socialists had urged for reducing inequalities. This Bismarckian nationalism was far removed from the spirit of the French Revolution, but the transformation had come about gradually.

Such a tragically transformed gospel of the French Revolution in both France and Germany was formulated dialectically by Henri Bergson, when he wrote in his *Two Sources of Morality and Religion:*

. . . in theory. . . . It [democracy] *proclaims* liberty, *demands* equality, and reconciles these two hostile sisters by reminding them that they are *sisters,* by exalting above everything fraternity. [Italics mine.—H.W.S.]

Here fraternity is enthroned, while liberty and equality are reduced to the status of two quarrelsome sisters who need a big brother to keep the peace.

Meanwhile a similar, though less thorough, corruption of the ideal of fraternity was taking place in Great Britain and the United States. Disraeli converted the British to an imperial fraternity, in which all British citizens could feel free to impose their freedom and their fraternity on their unequals among the "backward peoples," while at home the aristocrats could champion democracy at the expense of liberalism. In the United States Daniel Webster could proclaim, "Liberty and union, now and forever, one and inseparable," as though he were speaking in the Jeffersonian tradition, but everyone knew that in his mind liberty and equality were subordinated to union, if not actually separated from it. And in the country at large, while different interpretations of liberty and equality were tearing the country apart, the effort to preserve the union became increasingly nonfraternal and militant. Whether the preservation of the union can be called genuine "fraternity" is still an open question.

Further illustrations of this familiar story seem

unnecessary, for everyone knows that in various ways the revolutionary ideal of fraternity was transformed during the nineteenth century into the idol of national solidarity. And everyone knows that this degeneration of the ideal culminated in the tragedy of the First World War. No one would deny now that the nationalized version of fraternity served the political and economic interests of great powers and promoted their rivalry more than it promoted either liberty at home or equality among nations.

But fraternity has also been given an idealistic, religious formulation, less nationalistic but no less dangerous to liberty and equality. For example, the Italian philosopher Gioberti, in the midst of the struggle for Italian unification under liberal auspices, appealed to the papacy, which was then, as usual, deaf to liberalism. He tried to promote Italian solidarity on the ground that the Italians as a people have a moral, spiritual "primacy" or mission among peoples, and that they must be unified on the basis of the Catholic faith in universal brotherhood in order that they may fulfil their divine mission to spread fraternity abroad. Let the Roman Church, he argued, be mother to the Italian state, and let all Italians realize their essential unity, not in republican institutions or political liberty, but in spiritual fraternity. Of course, the Roman Church could not sacrifice its world-wide claim to catholicity for the sake of Italian unity; nevertheless, it listened attentively to Gioberti's doctrine of fraternity, as did Mussolini. Why should not the Vatican be world headquarters for the gospel of brotherhood? Let all men acknowledge the fatherhood of God and let this spiritual union of mankind be also the true expression of equality and freedom. It is in just these terms that the Pope is now appealing to all men to be brothers. Forget, he says, the revolutionary ideology which has fomented the spirit of class conflict and international rivalry. Submit to the law of peace and charity, practice justice, and teach each other the essential dignity of man and the equality of all before God.

Now that the secular, nationalistic version of fraternity has been driven to mad extremes by Hitler and Mussolini, this Roman Christian version has gained great power. Millions of Europeans are being told: you can and must postpone liberty and equality. The immediate, overwhelming issue is Marx vs. Christ! Choose now between class conflict and brotherhood! Just now there is no other alternative! It is neither necessary nor expedient to put this issue in terms of elaborate ideologies or philosophies of history. Common men need a democratic, common-sense appeal: Do you want class war or world fraternity? The Papal Encyclical *Divini Redemptoris*, which was promulgated during the depression, put this issue to the world simply and emphatically: a just social order must be based "on solidly Christian foundations." No brotherhood without submission to God. In the United States this Catholic appeal was popularized by Fulton J. Sheen, then not yet bishop, who in 1939 published his *Liberty, Equality and Fraternity*. In this book he linked the ideal of liberty with capitalism, equality with communism, and fraternity with Catholicism. Seldom has the Church been able to be a greater world power than today. And seldom has ecclesiastical politics been put so simply on a moral and religious basis. In recent years there have been Catholic statesmen, apostles of this Christian type of fraternity, in power in Austria, Belgium, France, Germany, Ireland, Italy, Luxembourg, the Netherlands, Portugal, and Spain, as well as in several Latin-American countries. In the major powers of this fraternity bloc the social democrats, that is, the parties that have kept alive the French Revolutionary ideology, are assigned a subordinate rôle. And, as a consequence, there is a widespread opinion that democracy itself has transferred its allegiance from the faith of the French Revolution to a "solidly Christian foundation." A single quotation from a typical expression of this doctrine must suffice:

When at the end of the eighteenth century the Rights of Man were proclaimed in America and in France, and the peoples bidden to partake of the ideal of Liberty, Equality and Fraternity, a great challenge was hurled into the whole political realm at the mighty of this world and at their experienced skepticism—hurled by the people, by the plain man, by the spirit of childhood and faith, and at the same time by an ideal of universal generosity. The evangelical impulse which thus erupted bore the imprint of a secularized Christianity; but rationalist philosophy added to it illusions, which soon became bloody, and which assured mankind that the goodness of nature and reason alone would suffice for the coming of the great promise of justice and peace. But through these illusions the heart of man sensed a sacred truth, that the energies of the Gospel must pass into temporal life. . . . It was Christianity that announced to the peoples the kingdom of God and the life to come; Christianity has taught them the unity of the human race . . . and the law of brotherly love which reaches out to all, even to those who are our enemies, because all men, to whatever social group, race, nation or class they may belong, are members of God's family and adopted brothers of the Son of God. . . . Friendship between citizens

cannot prevail in actual fact within a social group if a
stronger and more universal love, brotherly love, is not
instilled in it, and if civic friendship, itself becoming
brotherhood, does not overflow the bounds of the social
group to extend to the entire human race. . . . Not
only does the democratic state of mind stem from the
inspiration of the Gospel, but it cannot exist without it.
[Taken *passim* from Jacques Maritain's *Christianity and
Democracy*.]

This is a moderate and relatively philosophical version of the doctrine which is being preached today to
democrats of all nations: democracy is entirely dependent on the Christian gospel of brotherhood and
its religious sanction. Unfortunately for this gospel,
it has now become evident that to the "bloody illusions" of the Enlightenment and of the "secularized
conscience," we must add the no less bloody illusions
of Christian fraternity. For it is all too easy for men
to acknowledge a common Father and even a common "Mother Church" and yet not practice brotherhood in peace and justice.

But for those who still put their hope and trust
primarily in fraternity, it is true that the world headquarters of the faith have moved from Paris to Rome.
Civic virtue must now wear a clerical garb and speak
with supernatural authority. It does not seem plausi-

ble that the leaders of this faith will in the near future make their peace with "secularized consciences"
or even with non-Christian religious brotherhoods.

The second part of our story tells of the estrange-
ment of liberty and equality. How did Washington
become Liberty Headquarters? The story takes us
to the early days of the nineteenth century, for the
chief hope of liberty moved across the ocean long
before the Statue of Liberty did. We must go back
at least to De Tocqueville's voyage to America, in
the early days of the romantic enthusiasm. This liberal French nobleman had a very definite aim in
visiting America; he had a thesis to prove, and, as in
the case of most tourists, what he saw confirmed his
thesis. American life was supposed by him to exhibit
for the benefit of Europe the opposition between liberty and equality. He was willing enough to let
America go ahead on the road of equality to eventual
ruin, but he wished to warn Europe to cultivate
liberty and liberalism rather than equality and democracy. He summed up his position in the famous
dictum:

. . . the principle of equality begets two tendencies: the
one leads men straight to independence, and may sud-
denly drive them into anarchy; the other conducts them

by a longer, more secret, but more certain road to servitude.

In France De Tocqueville's distinction between liberty and equality made little impression, since it was already taken for granted, but in England it became the text for a series of criticisms of the French Revolutionary ideals, the upshot of which was to treat liberty and equality as antithetical ideas. Jeremy Bentham's liberalism had been conceived in the spirit of the Enlightenment and its rationalism. There was no theoretical problem about equality in his mind. He simply postulated as a basis for calculating general happiness: "Let each individual count for one and only one." The practice of "one man, one vote," which is now generally taken for granted as a moral principle and not merely as a convenient form of suffrage, was not established in British political practice, and Bentham made no attempt to defend it morally or to argue that men are equal. He was concerned not with voting devices but with a theory of happiness, and he stated without further argument that for the purposes of his calculations it was necessary that the happiness of one person be assigned value equal to the happiness of another. This seemed plain *equity* to him. When John Stuart Mill came to revise Bentham's utilitarianism, he undertook a more psychological approach to individuality. He had to rest his theory on the qualitative differences among pleasures and pains; different things make different persons happy in different ways. Hence, there was a fundamental parting of the ways between his liberalism, that is, his defense of individual liberty, and Bentham's egalitarian calculus. From then on, British bourgeois liberalism was frequently an opponent of the extension of the suffrage and of democratic theory in general. It was the protection of minorities against oppressive public opinion and against majority rule that became a major concern among British liberals.

The conflict in British thought came to a head in 1873, when Sir James Stephen published his *Liberty, Equality, Fraternity*. The author had served for a time on the Indian Viceroy's Commission and had become converted to the Indian idea of caste. In his famous book he argued that the social order must be based on the natural inequalities of men. In an ideal or well-classified society, he maintained, class distinctions would correspond to natural differences. In 1885 this argument was again put forward persuasively by the distinguished conservative jurist, Sir Henry Maine, who quoted Stephen with approval and concluded in general that liberty and equality are mutually exclusive ideals.

These ideas were quickly imported into the United States. Under the influence of Stephen and Maine, President A. Lawrence Lowell of Harvard University wrote in 1889 his influential treatise, *Essays on Government*. What he calls "the American System" is based not on equality, since equality tends toward socialism and paternalism, but on respect for personal liberty and private rights. The idea of the natural rights of man he calls an "exploded doctrine" and, basing his argument on the principles of Mill's utilitarianism, asserts that the general welfare is best promoted through economic liberty (which implies economic inequality). An individual, he says, must "be able to enjoy unmolested the fruits of his labor," no matter how large those fruits may be. But in a democracy the majority, who have little property, will try to equalize property by robbing the rich of their "fruits." Hence, liberty and equality are enemies to each other and one of the chief functions of the United States Constitution, he thought, is to restrain lovers of economic equality from undermining individual liberties.

Lowell's defense of liberty came two years after Edward Bellamy's *Looking Backward* (1887), but no one then suspected how popular Bellamy's appeal to equality would be. The socialist enthusiasm among the middle classes in the United States during

the eighteen nineties caused the liberals of the Lowell type to worry about the future of their "American
system." They became increasingly concerned in
1897 when Bellamy published his second book and
entitled it *Equality*. Here he openly challenged the
liberty-devotees by asserting that

equality is the vital principle of democracy. . . . Nothing can be in the long run . . . sound economics which
is not sound ethics. It is not, therefore, a mere coinci-
dence, but a logical necessity that the supreme word of
both . . . should be . . . equality. The golden rule
. . . is as truly the secret of plenty as of peace. . . .
The corner stone of our state is equality. . . . What is
life without its material basis, and what is an equal
right to life but a right to an equal material basis for it?

To this thesis President Nicholas Murray Butler, of
Columbia University, replied, "The corner-stone of
democracy is natural inequality, its ideal the selec-
tion of the most fit." Butler developed this doctrine
much as Lowell had done and published in 1907 his
True and False Democracy. He explained that the
only reason for political and legal equalities is that
they promote liberty. The only economic equality
tolerable is equality of opportunity, which he defines
as those conditions which are created by the state to
insure that each man's share of wealth is determined

solely by his natural abilities. And he said very pointedly, citing Lord Acton, "The deepest cause which made the French Revolution so disastrous to liberty was its theory of equality." In this same year, 1907, the arch laissez-faire liberal, William Graham Sumner, of Yale, published his famous *Folkways*. His summary statement of his dogmatic Darwinism is about as extreme a position on the antithesis between liberty and equality as possible:

The doctrine that all men are equal is being gradually dropped, from its inherent absurdity, and we may at any time find it expedient to drop the jingle about a government of the people, by the people, and for the people. . . . Competition is a law of nature. Nature is entirely neutral . . . If, then, there be liberty, men get from her just in proportion to their works. . . . Let it be understood that we cannot go outside of this alternative: liberty, inequality, survival of the fittest; not-liberty, equality, survival of the unfittest. The former carries society forward and favors all its best members; the latter carries society downwards and favors all its worst members.[1]

In 1924 ex-president Arthur T. Hadley, of Yale University, joined the presidents of Harvard and Columbia in defending economic liberty by expounding "The Conflict between Liberty and Equality," and in the course of his address he declared: "The signers of the Declaration of Independence themselves can hardly have meant what they said to be taken literally." [2] Equality, he argued, is an ideal for backward peoples; progressive peoples are committed to liberty and *more* liberty. When Prohibition came, these champions formed "The Liberty League" which campaigned not only for the repeal of Prohibition but also against the election of Franklin D. Roosevelt, taking up President Herbert Hoover's "challenge of liberty."

While conservative Republicans were thus making liberty undemocratic, the Democrats under Woodrow Wilson undertook to formulate a "new freedom." They, too, did not openly defend equality, but at least they did not regard liberty as in essential conflict with equality. The new freedom, they explained, would lessen inequalities without committing itself to equality. Finally Franklin D. Roosevelt gave the culminating touch to the development of the current American ideology by formulating his Four Freedoms. Something of the traditional doctrine of equality is incorporated into these "freedoms," also some fraternity; hence, this Four Freedoms slogan makes a convenient American substitute for "liberty, equality, and fraternity," liberty having more or less successfully swallowed up the other two.

Without explicitly repudiating the Four Freedoms, which have become the cornerstone of an American ideology, some adherents of the old Liberty League doctrine have tried to revive the popularity of "individual liberties." For example, in 1949 F. A. Harper published a book entitled *Liberty, a Path to its Recovery* (published for The Foundation for Economic Education) in which the problem is clearly stated as being one of restoring a lost liberty. "Liberties that have been taken away from individuals must be restored; there can be no other answer." And this, too, it seems, can be no answer! Liberty remains a basic problem for American government and morals.

Lastly, I must add a little more on the fortunes and misfortunes of the ideal of equality since the days of the French Revolution. The outline of this story during the nineteenth century has already been told in connection with the histories of fraternity and liberty, but it is necessary to explain in what sense Moscow may be regarded as Equality Headquarters. For the case of Moscow is not so clear. The very word "equality" seems to have been repudiated by the Bolshevist interpreters of Marx as being a remnant of bourgeois mentality. According to Stalin,

Whoever draws up wage-scales on the "principle" of equality and ignores the difference between skilled and

unskilled labor is at loggerheads with Marxism and
Leninism.

The sort of socialism in which everyone receives the
same wages, the same quantity of meat, the same quantity of bread, and receives the same kind of products—
such a socialism is unknown to Marxism. . . . Equalisa-
tion in the sphere of consumption and personal life is
reactionary petty bourgeois nonsense, worthy of some
primitive ascetics but not of a socialist society.[3]

However, though both the ideals of egalitarian
consumption and egalitarian rights are repudiated as
survivals from the bourgeois revolution, there is an
attempt to maintain a positive socialist theory of
equality. The chief text from Marx himself is con-
tained in his *Critique of the Gotha Program* (1875):

The right of the producers is proportional to the
amount of labor they contribute; the equality consists in
the fact that everything is measured by an equal measure, labor. . . . This equal right is an unequal right for
unequal work. . . . In a higher phase of communist
society, after the tyrannical subordination of individuals
according to the distribution of labor, and thereby also
the distinction between manual and intellectual work,
have disappeared, after labor has become not merely a
means to live but is in itself the first necessity of living,
after the powers of production have also increased and
all the springs of co-operative wealth are gushing more
freely together with the all-round development of the

individual, then and only then can the narrow horizon of bourgeois rights be left far behind, and society inscribe on its banner: "From each according to his capacity, to each according to his need."

In this text Marx is evidently passing from a literal application of equality to the socialist conception of equality as equity. The radical application of equity must be reserved for the full flowering of communism. Meanwhile, and this is the doctrine preached in Moscow, *labor* must serve as the measure of equality.

But equality has, in addition to this economic meaning, a revolutionary social meaning for Europeans: it means classless society. The abolition of feudalism is still fresh in the memories of Eastern Europeans, and the attempt to abolish even lesser class distinctions is still a serious concern for any socialist government. To be sure, this ideal of creating a classless society is also linked to the idea of comradeship or fraternity, but the distinctive Moscow variety of comradeship implies a combination of social equality with militant co-operation. Equality in arms in the service of future social equality clearly dominates the Soviet dictatorship of the proletariat. This militant equality is not only supreme, it definitely conflicts with less revolutionary conceptions of liberty and fraternity. Hence, it is no exaggeration to say that, as Washington gives pre-eminence to liberty, so Moscow gives pre-eminence to equality. In Washington equality is "under law" and in Moscow liberty is under arms, subjected to the requirements of the vanguard of the people's army in its struggle to bring the blessings of equality to the whole world. Thus the world is divided into a "freedom-loving" fraternity and an equality-hungry comradeship.

This historical sketch must suffice to indicate the general factors that transformed a well-rounded eighteenth-century world into the world triangle of today. This analysis, if it is substantially correct, should clarify the present conflict of ideals. The moral issues at stake are not those that divide East and West; it is not geographical distance that causes the trouble. The conflict is caused by a moral dis-integration in each people and each soul, by the gradual divergence of ideals that are by tradition parallel. We are living and thinking in three moral dimensions without making the necessary correla-tions, and hence we are doomed to confusion and collision. Here, as a moral analyst, I should end this diagnosis. But as a citizen among citizens and as a member of an emerging world community, I must raise the practical question, though I can shed little light upon it. What is to be done about it?

It would be much too simple to conclude that we must restore the old trinity, the three-in-one conception of our forefathers. As health cannot be restored by restoring youth, so history cannot be made by going into reverse. It is perfectly idle to try to persuade Washington, Moscow, and Rome of the truth of what I have been saying, for even if they were inclined to admit the theoretical truth of it, this confession would not convince them that they really belong together in one world today and would contribute little toward a plan of practical co-operation. The disintegration has gone too far. Representatives from the three angles of the triangle can meet to negotiate, but they cannot see eye to eye; they cannot appeal to the old ideology. They can make compromises in the interests of "co-existence," but they cannot meet on common ground or in doctrinal peace. Under these circumstances practical statesmen must build a new world without having a world order as a foundation. They must arrive at specific agreements patiently and hope that somehow a new order will emerge. It is this kind of reconstruction, we hope, that is going on at diplomatic conferences and in the councils and assemblies of the United

Nations. This process is much more than cold war; it is experimental repair work, patching up a world that is badly torn.

But we are here concerned not with the art of political construction through negotiation but with a more theoretical problem of moral science. Have we any reason for our hope that out of this process a genuine community of peoples can emerge? Is there evidence that the three traditional ideals are being reshaped in practical politics so that they are compatible in a new pattern of community? It would seem reasonable to look for such reshaping not in any of the three world headquarters which we have been considering but in other political centers, which may be emerging as new world centers. The detection of new world centers, of "new-look" communities, is largely guesswork. I shall mention three centers of experimentation that seem promising to me, but I may be looking in the wrong directions; prophecy has not been reduced to a science.

First, there is the experimentation in which the British people is now engaged. I believe that London is more of an ideological laboratory than is commonly supposed. The British are peculiarly exposed to the winds of doctrine that blow across the seas and channels from every direction, and they must erect their own security in the face of them, using all available resources in all kinds of ways. Hence their experiments in democracy, which are being conducted with exceptional good will, intelligence, and moral seriousness, should be instructive for the world. They are taking their experiences experimentally and are really learning, though it be the hard way. I quote a typical bit of current British moralizing, in order to give an example of both the earnestness and the vagueness of the present ideological research:

. . . the vision of a more democratic society (is) being attacked on the grounds that whilst liberty is a generous and expansive ideal, equality is an envious, covetous, restrictionist ideal; whereas these characteristics of equality have only been acquired incidentally during the process of social enactment, and are in no way intrinsic in the vision of democratic equality itself. A spirit of interdependence and co-operation is no more morally reprehensible than a spirit of independence and individual enterprise. Both can be reconciled within the many-sided activities of a democratic community of free and equal men. . . .[4]

. . . Within this society the ideal of equality, like the ideal of liberty, goes on being extended and refined, until it finds expression in a widening sphere of human activities. These activities include behaviour towards other communities, national or colonial, as well as domestic policies. Finally, from the new way of life thus engendered, a third kind of equality is born. It is a vision of that spontaneous quality of human relationships, undefined by social organisation, which characterises relations between members of the same family, and which the fathers of modern democracy called "fraternity." In modern history no large territorial community has yet reached that stage in any completeness, though glimpses of it appear in times of acute national crisis, and already the vision of such relationships has inspired men to action. . . .[5]

It is because the totality of the democratic ideal has been lost from sight, because one form of its manifold idealism has been treated as alone "fundamental" or "real" democracy, that it has been distorted and diverted from its path. Its path is the middle way of harmony and reconciliation. But to follow the middle way is not to defend patchwork compromise or lukewarm half-measures. If democracy be a middle way, it is in this more profound sense of a balanced movement of idealism and progress, satisfying the all-round, many-sided requirements of the human personality, both spiritual and material. It is no doubt over-simplification to say that western civilization, at last, is moving from the first phase, the fight for liberty, through the present stage of the quest for equality, and may eventually progress towards the ultimate goal of human fraternity. The democrat has some reason to believe that this movement is taking place, so long as the achievement of the progress is not assumed to be inevitable.[6]

This is a tentative, hesitant statement of an experimental ideology for democracy; democratic moral progress is conceived as having three stages: struggle for liberty, quest for equality, spirit of fraternity—a cumulative process toward "completeness" and "spontaneity."

Secondly, I would call attention to another center of public moral reconstruction—India. If I were attempting to be dialectical in my analysis, I would, of course, present India as Britain's "antithesis" or "negation." In India an amazing number of ideals and ambitions are struggling for realization. From the ancient Vedas, from modern Europe, from Russia, Africa, and China there are gathered around New Delhi a confused mass of diversified religious teachings, political ethics, and philosophies of history. India, perhaps more than any other country, is being compelled to evaluate in this dramatic, revolutionary crisis the various and conflicting ways of salvation, security, and emancipation. Like Great Britain, India is morally and politically in dead earnest. It is self-centered and yet an emerging world center, a cultural laboratory in which East and West, North and South, violence and nonviolence, equality and castes, are being tested by fire. Out of this seething mass there may come a new political and cultural compound which all peoples should study attentively, since it may throw much light on the complicated tasks of reconstruction that have been created for all of them by the present world ferment.

Lastly, I would call attention to the special commissions on human rights and related problems that are working in the framework of the United Nations and affiliated specialized agencies. They are making an effort through international co-operation to find a new moral center for mankind. They have formulated a universal declaration of human rights for our own time, and they are focusing the attention of all peoples on the common core of practical democracy to which liberty, equality, and fraternity must somehow be related if they and we are to survive. The United Nations and the UNESCO states may not be really united and certainly do not constitute a world government, but their efforts can nevertheless be an essential moral service. At the meetings of these bodies there assemble from the three corners of the political world representatives of the three angles from which any problem of public morals must now be approached, and there they are forced to turn their backs on their own angles and to focus their minds on the center toward which all are groping.

Though they may be long in finding that center, we ought not despair of their efforts so soon; rather we should be alert for all signs of convergence. Premature, opportunistic union now would be more futile than the laborious process of enduring even angry meetings of minds so long as there is a genuine seeking for enlightenment and peace.

However, it is not to these great public laboratories of reconstruction that I wish to call attention primarily. They are instructive only insofar as we can relate them to the conflicts and confusions in our own selves. The moral schizophrenia which most needs diagnosis and cure is the inner, intellectual corruption that we have undergone as persons in allowing ourselves to be carried away by diverging ideals. Our consciences are in peril when we pay lip service to three incompatible ideals. Liberty is in danger of going toward what Hobbes described as its inevitable culmination, "the war of all against all." Equality is in danger of sanctioning tyranny and cruelty, while fraternity is apt to cloak bigotry. The three ancient specters—war, tyranny, fanaticism— which have haunted the growth of civilization for ages have now returned to oppress us more savagely than ever. A generation ago we had been taught not to fear these ghosts of savagery; today we have learned, and not from books, that these terrors still lie ahead of us and threaten our ruin. Like the ancient Greeks we have achieved a high level of sophistication and art, and like them we have counted too much on courage to see us through. We, too, live in lands of the free and the brave, but we have nonetheless become fearful and insecure. To be alarmed at the inner disintegration of our public character is certainly a reasonable, wholesome fear. In our confused position it may be folly to conceal our insecurity by a faith in collective security. For the type of union in which there is strength is not a huddling together in fear. There must be an internal strength and integrity that is more than courage and more than mutual aid.

I turn, therefore, to what seems to me to be an urgent philosophical need of our time, the need for restoring in our own souls and in our polity an understanding of how our three traditional ideals can again be correlated. To do this I must examine the relations that obtain generally between rights and needs, and then I must ask what virtues are needed to keep these relations intact. I must analyze successively three dimensions of the moral order and their categories. Thus the pursuit of our practical problem should lead to a theoretical formulation of the elements of public ethics. I shall follow the conventional order: first, liberty, then equality, lastly fraternity. But as I go along I shall try to prove that no one of them is first or last, and that none can be maintained as an ideal without involving all three. Others may make of this a trinitarian mystery, if they wish, but I shall be content if what I have to say makes elementary good sense. After this introductory sermon, I shall turn to the language and habits of the schoolroom and trust that an academic restatement of fundamentals may also serve our need for inner fortification and public defenses.

2
LIBERTY
EQUITY
AND
HUMAN
RIGHTS

CHAPTER TWO

*La liberté, "ce nom terrible écrit sur le char des orages,"
est au principe de toutes les révolutions. Sans elle, la justice
paraît aux rebelles inimaginable. Un temps vient, pourtant,
où la justice exige la suspension de la liberté. La terreur,
petite ou grande, vient alors couronner la révolution. Chaque
révolte est nostalgie d'innocence et appel vers l'être. Mais la
nostalgie prend un jour les armes et elle assume la culpabilité totale, c'est-à-dire le meurtre et la violence. Les révoltes
serviles, les révolutions régicides et celles du XXᵉ siècle, ont
ainsi accepté, consciemment, une culpabilité de plus en plus
grande dans la mesure où elles se proposaient d'instaurer une
libération de plus en plus totale. Cette contradiction, de-
venue éclatante, empêche nos révolutionnaires d'avoir l'air
de bonheur et d'espérance qui éclatait sur le visage et dans
les discours de nos Constituants. Est-elle inévitable, carac-
térise-t-elle ou trahit-elle la valeur de révolte, c'est la question qui se pose à propos de la révolution comme elle se pose
à propos de la révolte métaphysique.*

—ALBERT CAMUS, L'Homme Révolté

T HE ancient Greeks regarded themselves as free when they were governed by laws and not by individuals. A Greek city-state was said to be free as a whole, in contrast to a "barbarian" kingdom. The law was believed to be divine and inherently worthy of respect. Similarly among the ancient Israelites the privilege of theocracy, of being chosen to be God's direct subjects, implied the direct revelation of the divine commands and a freedom from human sovereigns. The Romans, too, regarded law as sacred; to

47

be ruled by Roman law was at once a divine right, a Roman privilege, and a mark of a free man.

Today the law has lost almost all its sanctity and much of its dignity. It is all too human. A certain awe, to be sure, is inspired by the constitution of a country, and a judge still is peculiarly honorable as he states the law. But law in general brings to mind not the divine righteousness but the shifting and shifty processes of legislation and litigation. The story of how law came to lose its halo is too long for telling here. Hence, I begin by simply noting that in contemporary conduct the law is a commonplace thing, though in our classical heritage it is a sacred gift. It does not occur to us to look upon the laws as the very source of our freedom; on the contrary, we look upon the law as a restraint. When we respect the laws, we mean nothing more than to obey them. Whereas to respect them in the sense of doing them honor or even of bowing to them as divine seems to us an attitude unworthy of free men, who are desirous of being self-governing. But as we reflect and compare our attitudes with those of our ancestors, we realize at once that this modern sense of being equal to or better than our laws puts us in a critical position. To grasp the full force of this cultural and civic turning point we must explain, if we can, under what circumstances today law still receives respect; or, negatively, under what circumstances men lose the faith that their laws are the substance of their freedom.

Englishmen will never forget the famous complaints of the Independents during the Puritan Revolution, when they cried out against Parliament:

Truly it is a sad thing, but too true, a plain quiet-minded man in any place in England is just like a harmless sheep in a thicket, can hardly move or stir, but he shall be stretched and lose his wool.[1]
Oh Englishmen! Where is your freedom? And what is become of your Liberties and Privileges that you have been fighting for all this while? [2]

The pathetic nature of these cries comes out clearly in Overton's *Remonstrance to Parliament,* when he writes, "We must therefore pray you to make a law against all kinds of arbitrary government." [3]

But let me recall also the classic American posing of this problem. When Thomas Jefferson, as a faithful disciple of Montesquieu, refused to support the Federal Constitution unless it included a bill of rights, he explained his fears by saying that "the tyranny of legislatures" must be met by putting a "legal check" in the hands of the judiciary, which, "if rendered independent and kept strictly to their own department, merits great confidence for their learning and integrity." [4] To which Alexander Hamilton replied that bills of rights

have no application to constitutions professedly founded upon the power of the people, and executed by their immediate representatives and servants. Here, in strictness, the people surrender nothing. . . . the Constitution is itself, in every rational sense, and to every useful purpose, A BILL OF RIGHTS. [5]

Note the irony of politics here: Jefferson is using the classical argument in appealing to law and reason to check the passions of legislatures and of men generally; whereas Hamilton, who himself shared this ancient faith in law, argued like a radical democrat that when the people are in power they need no rights to protect them against their own laws. Were these two founding fathers alive today and aware of the experience we have had with the Constitution and the Bill of Rights, they would probably join us in questioning both these arguments. Experience has taught us that constitutional law alone is not a sufficient safeguard of liberty, and that even bills of rights in the hands of the courts often fail to operate in the way in which they were intended to operate. Wherein, then, shall freemen put their faith? In right or in rights? In courts or in declarations? In the principles of justice or the love of liberty?

I shall not review the long debates on this first of all questions in political morality but shall state at once the conclusion which I wish here to defend. I believe that declarations of rights are useful both as expressions of the love of liberty and as formulations of public conscience, and that lawyers, judges, and legislators are respected by their fellow-citizens only insofar as their conduct of the law serves to implement or embody rights. Rights, in short, are morally basic to legal right.

By "public conscience" I mean the judgment made by members of a community concerning those social relations which they wish to encourage by their institutions and those which they wish to discourage. The public conscience is not identical with a common sense of values or agreement on common goods. It has a more restricted scope; it seeks to define the realm of public relations and vested interests; that is, those human relations and interests which are to be maintained and those which are to be abolished *by institutional agreements*. Among such institutional agreements the legal system or juridical order is prominent, but it is nevertheless only one of several.

There are also the systems of exchange, of communication, of family life, of public worship, of arts and sciences, sports and wars. Even if we admit that the legal system serves to keep these other systems "in order," it seems idle to insist that it or two or three of these social systems are fundamental. Whether in our philosophy we glorify the family, or the law, or the army, or the church, as the ultimate source of authority in public life, we must all agree that in practice we share a number of these vested interests, and that together they constitute our institutional order or community structure. The number and interrelation of these corporate interests varies from time to time and from culture to culture. But no single institution is comprehensive or constitutionally ultimate. The ultimate appeal is to what I have called the public conscience. When it makes a declaration of rights, it attempts to determine the social relations which shall obtain among these systems of interests. Rights, therefore, are not merely norms for law but for institutions generally; they measure the rightness or justice of all our institutions. They are a general guide for politics, economics, organized religion, in short, for public morality and policy. Accordingly, it is not only our legal system that gains or loses public respect according to whether it favors or violates our declared rights; it is our culture as a whole that is subject to the judgment of such declarations.

 But the question still remains: Why do we call such norms "rights" or "liberties"? This question deserves a serious answer but seldom receives it. Most of our answers reflect impatience: we are more interested in asserting our rights than in explaining what constitutes a right. Let us consider three of the theories that are current.

According to one theory, very widely preached today, the most basic rights are inherent in man; they are supposed to be the inalienable possessions of individuals. The theological version of this idea is that man is "endowed by his creator" with certain rights, called "natural" or "inalienable" to distinguish them from civil rights, which are legal and which therefore depend on legal systems. One such right, for example, is "life." Now what do we assert, when we declare that we have a "right to life"? Do we mean that the world owes us a living? Or do we assert that our neighbors owe us a living? Or do we mean that all life is sacred and should be inviolate in the sense that it is wrong to kill, though it may not be wrong to let die? Or do we believe that human beings have a peculiar dignity which entitles them to respect simply because they are human beings? One recent attempt to answer this question reads as follows:

> The right to live is the condition and, as it were, the foundation of all other rights. It is the condition of other rights since it is the minimum human right. It is inseparably involved in the very existence of man. But to live is more than barely to exist, and it is therefore the right which makes specific all other rights since they mark the degree of well-being which man may achieve. All rights derive, on the one hand, from the nature of man as such and, on the other, since man depends on man, from the stage of development achieved by the social and political groups in which he participates.[6]

Even this cautious statement is not unambiguous: "to live is more than to exist"; "the right to live" is not a particular right, but "the condition and foundation of all rights"; "it is the minimum human right," deriving "on the one hand, from the nature of man" and "on the other, . . . from the groups in which he participates." These statements are not strictly compatible as elements of a definition: this right is not a particular right, and yet it is a right; it defines a minimum, but not so low as bare existence; it derives both from nature and from society. But in a vague way these statements try to suggest that there is something in the "nature of man as such" that entitles him to recognition by his fellow men as something to let live.

To believe in natural rights in this vague way seems innocent enough—a mere minimum of humaneness and decency. It seems ungenerous to quarrel with men who believe that we have the right to live. As an article in a church's social creed it might pass unchallenged. But philosophers cannot let it stand as an ultimate ground of justification. It is dubitable and dubious. I shall not review the familiar arguments but concentrate attention on the question whether a right is based on something inherent in any individual, or whether it defines social relations. The conclusion to which I have come is that any right, even the right to live, is predicated of a man not in view of his nature or essence but in view of his cultural context. Rights are cultural, not natural. That is to say, a man asserts not his own inherent dignity when he asserts his so-called right to life, liberty, and the pursuit of happiness; he makes a *demand* to be *considered* as a worthy member of a community, unless he makes it difficult for others to live in the community. "Live and let live" is a minimum element of sociability, and implies no judgments about human nature or inherent dignity. If certain rights are inalienable, it is because they are essential to social life. That life is essential to a human individual's existence is a proposition scarcely worth asserting. The *right to* life is not based on this evident fact but on a policy of broad tolerance. Hence, a "natural" or "inalienable" right is a right that is natural or essential to society. However, it is not necessary to believe that there are certain rights that are universally necessary for all societies. In any society certain rights are essential to it, but these rights may vary widely with the variety of societies and their varied natural environments. Thus, a "universal declaration" of human rights may be compatible with a considerable cultural relativity; it does not necessarily assert universal rights. The declaration is universal in the sense that the peoples or nations that are making the declaration are all agreed that their societies must respect these rights. The conscience of a community of nations may appeal to "the opinion of mankind" even if there is no universal opinion. The preamble of the United Nations' Universal Declaration, though it begins in the style of the classical mythology, "Whereas recognition of the inherent dignity and of the equal and inalienable rights of all members of the human family," proceeds in a different tone and asserts not that these rights are "self-evident" but that "this *recognition*" is "the foundation of freedom, justice and peace in the world" and "essential to promote the development of friendly relations between nations." Here the purpose of the declaration is clear, though the theory is still confused: the most essential factor in the effort to create a world community is the recognition of *the foundations of universal freedom, justice, and peace,* namely, the so-called inherent, equal, inalienable rights of all men, not as individuals, but *as members of the human family.* This language recalls the incidental phrase of the American preamble, "in order to form a more perfect union." The Universal Declaration is at the basis of a plan to form a more perfect union, and this plan rests not on a particular belief about human nature or about the origin of rights but on a desire to create freedom, justice, and peace throughout the world. The aims of the eighteenth-century declarations were the reverse: they were intended to create national communities of *citizens,* but they asserted the rights of all *men* and appealed to "the opinion of mankind" in order to give a classical sanction to their revolutionary communities. The ideology of rights in the eighteenth century was based on cosmo-politanism; the anthropo-politan ideas of today and the appeal to "the human family" are likewise a mythology used to express an actual effort at universal union.

According to another theory of rights, a declaration of rights is an attempt to define the essential conditions of liberty, the supposition being that a general framework of liberty is the only possible ground for a growth of equality and fraternity. This theory makes liberty fundamental absolutely. There is an opposite theory according to which the primary condition of social life is man's recognition of his duty, either as a general framework of loyalty or as a system of particular obligations. Some say that man owes duties first to God, then to himself, and lastly to others. Whatever the origin of duties, however, once such a context of obligation is admitted, the recognition of rights can be explained and justified as the *means* whereby duties are fulfilled. Here liberties are justified not absolutely, but as implementations of equality and fraternity. But, thus to make either liberty or duty fundamental to the other makes neither intelligible; at least so it seems to me, though most theorists seem to think that the alternative is inescapable. I should think that liberty and duty explain each other only when taken strictly as correlatives and not one as the means to the other. If I claim a liberty as a right or privilege, I imply that someone has the duty of respecting this claim. One man's liberty is another man's duty. Freedom and obligation develop together. Once a liberty is conceived as a right it is moralized, that is, it is conceived as publicly recognized, an obligation among members of a community. If we admit that rights are social or public, we need not stop to debate which comes first or last, liberty or duty. Any right is both a liberty and a duty, and either taken out of the context of a public community becomes a mystery.

There is a third type of theory which assumes that a declaration of rights is also a confession of basic values, and that hence a universal declaration of rights is the expression of a faith in a universally valid scale of values. According to this theory, there is no difference between a declaration of the public conscience and a public confession of faith. This raises a large issue, which I cannot discuss fully here. Leaving aside the question of whether men have or should have universal or common values, and admitting that there are some value judgments in any declaration of rights, I think it is nevertheless important not to confuse a right and a value. By a "value" we generally mean something sought after, an end or good. A right is not a value in this sense.

Freedom, for example, is commonly desired and is usually regarded as a basic value. But a liberty in the sense of a right is not necessarily a good; it is a moral bond or relationship regarded as necessary for a good life, but in itself it is neither an intrinsic good nor a necessary evil. Individuals differ in their attitudes toward moral relationships or agreements, and the same individual may regard different relationships very differently, tolerating some as necessary nuisances and enjoying others as opportunities. But moral bonds, whether we regard them with Hobbes as substitutes for the sacrifice of "natural liberty" or with Aristotle as a form of friendship, are in their own nature neither goods nor evils—they are elements of reciprocity. Reciprocity may be enjoyed or hated, but a certain amount of it is accepted by most men as an obvious public convenience. If my neighbor and I make an agreement that when we pass each other we go to the right rather than to the left and not as we happen to please, we are apt to accept this as a *modus vivendi,* as a general device for avoiding particular collisions, and as being, in this utilitarian sense, a good idea. But the obligation or privilege (as you please) of going to the right is not inherently a good or value, in the sense that it is an enjoyable performance. In the same way rights and duties are common conveniences, useful because general and public, but they need not be in any further sense either good or evil. Viewed in this light, it is quite intelligible to say that liberties, duties, and rights determine basic structures or conditions of society, without implying any doctrine whatsoever concerning the scale of values in general.

A more genuine problem is raised by those theorists who, regardless of the more general problem of universal values, insist that human rights are directly related to human needs. To agree offhand, as some glibly do, that we have a right to whatever we really need, takes too much for granted. To say, on the other hand, that rights and needs are not intrinsically related seems even more arbitrary. It is difficult and hazardous to give a serious reply to this question without examining both rights and needs in some detail, for this question seems to be more of a practical than a philosophical problem. I shall, therefore, revert to this question after having discussed more particularly rights and needs. But first, I must examine some of the philosophical problems that arise when we try to relate human rights to human personality, to law, and to justice.

Lawyers have distinguished four classes of rights: (1) personal rights, (2) rights of men in their most general relations with other men, (3) public, civil, or political rights, and (4) economic or social rights. Into the technical legal values of these distinctions we need not enter, nor into the historical considerations which may explain this terminology. It is necessary here only to criticize the ways in which these distinctions have been carried over into the philosophies of rights. On the basis of the criticisms which we have made above and in view of the conclusion to which we came, that rights define social relations, we must say that *all rights are both social and personal.* It may be possible to conceive Robinson Crusoe's rights and duties to himself, to animals, or to his creator; but they are evidently more speculative than his duties to his man Friday. I am inclined to think that such rights and duties as are supposed to lodge even in a solitary individual are really, though indirectly, social, involving an unrecognized extension or projection of social relations to other beings or to possible, imagined communities; but I do not wish to argue the point, since it has little bearing on the rights commonly included in public declarations. Let us, therefore, omit reference to rights that are merely personally and privately acknowledged, and discuss rights that are explicitly personal, social, and public.

All rights are personal in the sense that they are meaningful only to a being that can make claims or demands. A person, as Gabriel Marcel has well emphasized, is an appropriator, a proprietor in the sense of being able to make things his own, and hence to claim them. A right is a kind of property or propriety, and to be really a *bearer* of rights one must be competent to claim-as-one's-own. This ability to appropriate, which is the ultimate basis of social individuality as well as of property, this "having" things or ideas in the sense of "holding on to" them (to use Aristotle's term), must be presupposed in any theory of rights. It is often referred to as man's inherent freedom or dignity; more accurate would be the reference to man's responsiveness or social sensitivity, which is the ultimate basis of his capacity for responsibility. Human freedom and dignity are resultants of this capacity. Hence one is putting the cart before the horse when one rests the case for rights and liberties on some hypothetical inherent freedom or dignity in human nature. The capacity to bear, to hold, to claim, which is the essence of personality, is the power which brings to man the qualities of freedom and dignity. It is not necessary here to discuss the notion of "corporate personality," but I ought to point out in passing that it is more than a legal fiction to regard a responsible corporation as a person. A corporation that has property and other rights is by no means an impersonal being. It is not only composed of persons, but it has a personality structure, involving collective duties, rights, decisions, actions, and rewards and punishments. It is such *moral* personality that is the essential factor for a theory of rights and duties. A living being may be a biological individual or organism long before he is a moral person; he may be human without having the "dignity" of a person. It is, therefore, more accurate to speak of "personal" than of "human" rights. But it is usually understood, in spite of the inaccurate terminology, that in this context we are speaking of human *persons*, either biological or institutional.

Secondly, all rights are social in the sense that they define claims made reciprocally. To assert a claim or obligation is an idle boast or gesture if it does not involve recognition of mutual, social respect for rights. Or, more abstractly, the assertion of rights and the respect for rights must be inalienable. They are two aspects of a single act or relationship. Hence the having or bearing of rights is not a self-created privilege or burden. No one can create a right for himself. Rights are reciprocally generated; they must be granted as well as asserted. It takes two to agree as well as to disagree, and all agreements are obviously social. Rights are *explicitly* agreements. They are more genuinely agreements than laws are, for laws can be imposed unilaterally by a government. A law may rest solely on power, not on reciprocity, and hence, to repeat an important point of this analysis, a right by its nature must be respected, whereas a law need not be. Ideally, to be sure, laws should approach the status of rights; but actually a law may rest on coercion, whereas an imposed right or duty is not genuine. Thus the existence of rights and duties adds a moral context to politics. It may not be necessary to assume a general social agreement or will to respect agreements in general as the logical ground of any particular right or duty. But this classical theory is still widely held. It is necessary, however, that any particular right have its moral ground in consent. The universal "logical" ground is really a mythical justification or sanction, for ultimately the so-called general social contract needs the same ground of reciprocity that any particular agreement needs. Certainly, any genuine right or duty must be inherently as respectable as the social contract is supposed to be. In effect, what the social contract theory does is to exploit the respectability of explicit agreements in order to cloak particular *laws,* which may not be respectable, with the moral garb of rights.

Thirdly, all rights are public in the sense that they must be openly held by a group as a part of that group's structure. Just as it takes more than one person to arrive at an agreement, so it takes explicit, public recognition and definition to establish a right or obligation that has a juridical status. There is no sense in regarding a right as a private possession inherent in a single person. To be a member of a juridical community is to be in public, for such membership must be claimed and granted on the basis of the reciprocal admission of particular rights and duties. No right stands alone. It is part of a community structure or "body of liberties." I am not asserting that this body of rights is the very essence or "constitution" of social life, though this is a classical doctrine. The theory of rights is not a general theory of society. What needs to be asserted is that whether or not a group has a biological existence in natural gregariousness, or an emotional bond of friendship, or some other uncovenanted ground, a community becomes a public body when the *concordia* or natural agreement which may have given it life generates an open, conscious recognition of rights or liberties.

Now, admitting these three assertions as a general theory of rights, that all rights are personal, that they are social, and that they are public, we can reconsider the four traditional classes of rights and attempt a more precise statement of the differences that distinguish them. The four types of rights that should be distinguished in practice are:

(1) *Basic community rights.* These might also be called "the general principles of fraternity"; they correspond roughly to what are called "personal" or "human" rights—*les droits des hommes.* These rights should be recognized in any group as necessary elements of mutual respect. For example, the assertion that no one has a right to hold slaves is simply a negative way of saying that all members of a community have some rights. No one can own another *person* rightly. To prohibit cruelty is to say that, as a general principle, all persons "have a right to life, liberty, and the pursuit of happiness" (though this popular formula is vague indeed). It is impossible to define precisely what we mean by cruelty and "mental cruelty," because its practical application varies so from culture to culture and from time to time. Though any civilized conscience has in it a hatred of cruelty, torture, and inhumanity, it takes

much legislation and moral criticism to give it precise and public meaning. But to proclaim this hatred in advance of legal specification is an intelligible act and a safeguard to decency. To assert that "everyone has the right to freedom of thought, conscience and religion, opinion and expression, peaceful assembly and association" likewise applies to any community in which mutual respect prevails. Such respect for persons does not necessarily involve a respect for life as such, in a purely biological sense, though many humanitarians feel such a respect and wish to extend to all animals the principles of "humaneness." It is not necessary to believe that all life is sacred, because one proclaims that all persons are inviolable. The inviolability with which we are here concerned as a moral principle does not rest on a quality in human nature but on a perception of rightful social relations. This is, to be sure, a debated question, and I know that many moralists have insisted that any living human organism is inviolable, and some have extended this principle to all life, notably Albert Schweitzer and the Brahmans and the Buddhist monks. Most men seem to be averse to cruelty, when others are practicing it, and would therefore be obligated, if they have a moral conscience, to refrain from cruelty themselves. Nevertheless, it seems to me that what is really essential to the *right* is not so much the mere expression of this general hatred of cruelty, as the obligation to refrain from cruelty towards members of a community. It is the community that thus asserts its dignity, and not the individual who thus boasts his native endowments.

(2) *Civil or political rights.* These are the technical rights of citizens. They are declared to be basic to a particular kind of community, namely, the commonwealth, the society of reciprocal government and law. What is commonly and somewhat pompously called self-government should more accurately be called reciprocal government. The Roman term, *res publica,* which underlies much of our political terminology, is itself vague. At least it has become increasingly vague in modern times, on account of the many meanings attached to "public" and to "people." But, in connection with the definition of civil rights, it is well to use the term "commonwealth" to denote a particular kind of public or association, namely, the society of law and government, rather than to denote the whole community or society. For the political order is today a less inclusive concept than it was in ancient Greece and Rome. Accordingly, civil or political rights are supposed to define the general conditions under which the administration of the com-

monwealth will be free and fair. In the interests of freedom and justice a commonwealth must publish the principles of government which it respects. These civil rights were the first to be proclaimed formally, as "petitions of right" or "bills of rights," and are an essential part of a free constitution, since they are basic norms for law. Among the most common civil rights are:

The law is no respecter of persons; any person is equally entitled to be governed by general laws.

No one shall be subjected to arbitrary arrest, detention, or exile.

Everyone is entitled to fair trial before an impartial tribunal.

No one shall be subject to arbitrary interference with his privacy, home, family, correspondence, honor, or reputation.

Everyone has the right to own property.

Every adult has the right to participate in government.

Such rules are generally regarded as necessary to political freedom and to legal justice. But, though they are essential principles of commonwealth, they are not sufficient to insure freedom and justice in the community as a whole. Hence it is important to note that they are merely civil or political rights and that the body politic is itself only one institutional structure of several that constitute a community. If I may paraphrase Hobbes against his own theory, I would maintain that any body politic that imagines itself to be the whole community is apt to become a Leviathan, for the commonwealth is not the total structure of society.

(3) *Workers' or producers' rights.* These are commonly called "economic rights." They define the basic conditions of co-operative production. Here there is less agreement than in the field of civil rights, but among the workers' rights that are commonly accepted are:

The right to "social security."
The right to work.
The right to "equal pay for equal work" or some other formula for fair wages.
The right to periodic rest and leisure.
The right of an individual to "form and join trade unions for the protection of his interests."
The right to a "healthy" standard of living.

Such principles, though they be publicly proclaimed, fall short obviously of the precision that legal norms should have; but so do the above named civil rights. They achieve precision through legislation and jurisdiction. The declaration of economic rights is a polemical subject, however, not so much

because of the difficulties of precision as because of
the varying methods of enforcement. On the one extreme are those economic rights that are closest to
civil rights and most adapted to judicial procedure,
and on the other extreme are those rules of co-operative production and distribution that are usually
enforced by nongovernmental methods and that may
even be regarded as "natural laws." The basic moral
question is to what extent the norms of production
can be assimilated to the principles of just administration. But whether the rights of production can be
interpreted as civil rights or not, it is morally and
socially important that they be proclaimed as worthy
of public respect. Lawyers naturally smile at rights
that cannot be incorporated into law nor brought
into court. And the rich naturally smile (though
nervously) when the poor appeal to "fair play," for
they observe that in any game or market some must
win and others lose. But genuine workers are apt to
agree that some principles of fair play in economic
processes must be established somehow, if the competition for commodities is not to be an outright
struggle to the death (or, as it is euphemistically
called, "a struggle for existence"). Hence there is a
general moral importance and meaning cognizable
in the declaration of economic rights, regardless of

the more technical question of the relation of these rights to law.

(4) *Rights of more specialized institutions and associations.* The political and economic bodies of rights fall midway between the most general community rights and the most technical rights of specialized societies. Though we have insisted that the political and economic structures are not all-inclusive, total orders, we must admit that they are readily distinguished from the so-called "private" associations. These latter associations, sometimes referred to vaguely as "cultural" institutions, are not completely private, and their rights become more or less involved in legislation and litigation. Among these "cultural" rights, or rights of specialized institutions, are: professional codes, religious orders, educational standards, linguistic conventions, copyrights, family prerogatives, and polite manners. These are seldom introduced into bills of rights and general declarations, but they are of great importance, nevertheless. Their variety is eloquent testimony of the wide range of our public concerns. I might mention a few that have found their way into the Universal Declaration of the United Nations:

Men and women of full age . . . have the right to marry and found a family.

Technical and professional education shall be made generally available to all on the basis of merit.

Education shall be directed to the full development of the human personality.

Parents have a prior right to choose the kind of education that shall be given their children.

Everyone has the right freely to participate in the cultural life of the community, to enjoy the arts and to share in scientific advancement and its benefits.

Every author has the right to the protection of the moral and material interests resulting from his authorship.

We have now distinguished roughly four classes of rights in terms of the particular types of community structures to which they belong. But it is difficult to dissociate such a classification entirely from the more practical classification of rights in terms of the ways in which they are enforced or regulated. A right is almost inevitably and immediately associated with government. In fact, those who have a practical concern for rights are apt to be impatient with any inquiry into the *nature* of rights which does not use as a criterion the mode of regulation. Nevertheless, I have intentionally subordinated the pragmatic criterion to the material one because of the great variety of systems of regulation to which, from time to time and from culture to culture, any one type of right may be subjected. However, now, having attempted to examine rights for what they are, we might consider a few rough generalizations concerning the mechanisms by which they operate at present and make their power felt.

(1) The most general rights are considered to be first of all standards of decency, good manners, or elementary morals. They are regarded as primarily matters of "conscience"; but they are often included in the preambles of constitutions and legal bills of rights. Religious bodies usually try to regulate "cases of conscience." Violation of these rights may be punished legally, but on the grounds of "public order and decency."

(2) Civil rights usually take their place in constitutional law and are enforced politically.

(3) Economic rights are subject both to "direct action" or collective bargaining and to political action or legislation.

(4) Specialized rights are usually left to the "self-regulation" of professional bodies, voluntary agreements, regulations for members of particular corporations, orders, or other associations.

The general conclusion which I wish to suggest on the basis of these commonplace observations is that it is useless to try to determine on general principles which rights should be legal rights and which should be left to other types of control. It is not even easy to determine which rights are as a matter of fact legal rights. This is especially true in the field of international law. Thus the right to basic education, which is now almost universally declared, might be interpreted to belong to any one of the four classes. Similarly, the right to own property. However, our chief concern here is not with the technical problems of classification but with the moral problem of determining *to whom* declarations of rights are addressed. It seems to me that our analysis makes abundantly plain that those rights that are unmistakably addressed to lawyers and legislators are surrounded on all sides by other rights which are addressed to the public conscience of a particular community or of all communities. It will not do for lawyers and legislators to say that these other rights are not addressed to them, for it is the whole body of rights that must be taken as the frame of reference for legal justice. Whether they are political rights or not, all declared rights serve to express publicly the full meaning of freedom and justice. Though a "universal declaration" is presumably addressed to all men, it is to public officials that such a declaration comes with a special warning: they have been notified what kind of a *social* order the *juridical* order is expected to serve, and therefore they have no excuse if men cease to respect their laws because they fail to promote these rights.

Such norms must have more than legal validity; they must honestly reflect a public conscience. But the public and the conscience to which a particular declaration belongs are not easily located. Usually a declaration involves what the drafters of the American Declaration of Independence called "a decent respect for the opinion of mankind," which means that there is a desire to appear respectable in a world community. The more ancient formula for making solemn declarations "under God" has the same appeal to a universal judgment. Thus, there is an element of universality or world community implied in most declarations of rights, especially when the declaration contains rights that are general for any type of community. The rights which we have classified under type I are general in the same sense that a law should be general—applying equally to any person—but they may also be conceived as being "universal" because they are intended to express the conscientious bonds of all men who have an interest in a universal community. It is, of course, difficult to believe that there actually exists a universal conscience by which all mankind is bound together into a fraternity, but the appeal to this ideal and the expression of such a hope are not meaningless gestures. Admitting that the moral public cannot be located with a precision that would satisfy lawyers, we must also admit that the moral public is wider than any legal community or any actual system of positive or common law.

In short, the conclusion to which I come is that the law is not morally sovereign or ultimate. And most framers of constitutions seem to be aware of this fact when they compose preambles and attach bills of rights. It is precisely in those states to which the old republican formula, *Lex rex,* applies, that there exists an undefined, changeable context or consciousness of rights or liberties to which the law is as really responsible as the government is responsible to law. The only power that this conscience wields is the power of judgment; it has no police power, but neither has the Supreme Court. The first essential of liberty is as plain and public a declaration of rights as circumstances permit, in order that the world may know in what terms justice is being conceived. The second essential is the ability to hold the juridical order responsible to them. Since bills of rights are thus a necessary foundation for liberty, they should not be condemned merely because they are not from the start embodied in the law of the land. Though they be *obiter dicta* or "transcendental nonsense" to lawyers, they may nevertheless prove their power by informing lawyers of their responsibilities to the community. It is prudent even for a lawyer to know a little jurisprudence in addition to the law.

Declarations of rights are, of course, particularly appropriate in situations where a new body of law is beginning to take shape. I have been referring chiefly to the United Nations' declaration, since this declaration is the most conspicuous recent example in the field of international law. In this field it is peculiarly important to have a formal statement of principles, for such a statement at once makes evident where the great gaps in international law are to be found. The great distance between the ideals respected by the international conscience and the actual controls exercised by international courts should not be interpreted as evidence of hypocrisy or as proof of the futility of international government. Declarations may be hypocritical, of course, but there is no reason for suspecting them of being so *in principle*. To be genuine and useful a declaration of rights should reflect an *actual* conscience and a *possible*, desirable legal order. A "realistic" statesman is overdoing his realism when he refuses to subscribe to any declaration of rights which cannot be immediately enforced as law; for he is expected to recognize, and recognize publicly, the imperfections of actual law when judged morally, and he should not be ashamed to show that he makes moral judgments. Since I have concentrated on the needs of international law at present, I ought to add some illustrations from current national constitutions. The preambles of the recent French and Indian constitutions contain good illustrations of the relation that obtains between a public commitment to rights and a constitutional framework of law.

The Preamble to the 1946 Constitution of the French Republic contains the following declarations:

The French people again proclaims that every human being, without distinction of race, religion or belief, possesses inalienable and sacred rights. It solemnly reaffirms the Rights and Liberties of Man and Citizen enshrined in the 1789 Declaration of Rights. . . . It proclaims in addition, as being particularly needed in our times, the following fundamental political, economic and social principles:

In all legal relations women are guaranteed rights equal to those of men.

Any person persecuted for liberty's sake has a right to asylum on French territory.

Everyone has the right to work and to obtain employment. No one may be hindered in his work or employment because of his origin, opinions or beliefs.

Everyone may defend his rights and interests through union activities and may join whatever union he pleases.

The right to strike is recognized, subject to legal regulation.

Every worker, through his representatives, takes part in collective agreements concerning working conditions as well as concerning the management of the business. When the exploitation of any resource or the conduct of any business assumes the character of a public service or of a de facto monopoly, it should become public property.

For every individual and family the nation provides the conditions necessary to growth. . . .

The French Republic, true to its traditions, obeys the rules of international law. It will not go to war for conquest nor ever use its forces against another people's freedom.

France agrees, insofar as others agree also, to limit its sovereignty when that is necessary for organizing or defending the peace.

The new Constitution of India is still more detailed and systematic in its declaration of principles. The Preamble pays its respects to the revolutionary tradition by asserting that this constitution aims "to secure to all its citizens: *Justice,* social, economic and political; *Liberty* of thought, expression, belief, faith, and worship; *Equality* of status and of opportunity; and to promote among them all *Fraternity*, assuring the dignity of the individual and the unity of the Nation." Part III enumerates the following "fundamental rights":

1. The right to equality, that is, no discrimination on grounds of caste or religion, abolition of untouchability and of titles, equality of opportunity.
2. The right to freedom. Under this head are included the usual civil liberties.
3. The right against exploitation. No slavery, forced labor or child labor.
4. The right to freedom of religion.
5. Cultural and educational rights. No discrimination in schools; respect for minority languages.
6. The right to own property.
7. The right to constitutional redress through a supreme court.

These fundamental rights are to be legally enforced; they constitute a formal bill of rights. But in addition, Part IV, there follow twelve "directive principles of state policy." These principles have neither the precision nor the legal force of rights but are nevertheless formulated in the Constitution as recognized ideals or norms for public policy. They state public needs rather than legal rules. They are (summarized):

1. The people's welfare demands provision for the means of livelihood, distribution of commodities for the common good, equal pay for equal work, a public health service, protection of women and children.
2. Villages should have local self-government.
3. All citizens have a right to work.
4. All citizens have a right to a living wage.
5. Laws must be uniform.
6. Education is compulsory.
7. The weaker castes and tribes must be protected.
8. Intoxicating liquors should be prohibited.
9. Scientific agriculture must have public support.
10. Monuments must be preserved.
11. The judiciary should be independent.
12. Peace and international law are to be upheld.

To legal ears such grandiose declarations may sound like mere declamations. But it is both unjust and foolish to be deaf to them. Such efforts to portray the conditions essential to freedom, though they may never be fully realized, may be honest expressions of an actual conscience, and one should never underestimate the power of a conscience. Here something is being held sacred to which the law itself must pay its respects. And this sacred body of rights is not so much an icon, enshrined, as it is a living and growing attribute of human beings. Reassertions of rights bring about revisions in view of new forms of slavery or opportunities for freedom. This sacred body of rights is "constitutional" not in the sense that it is constitutive of the state but that it is part of the "nature" or culture of the members of the nation; it is not a foundational platform, but a living growth. In short, in opposition to legalistic theories of so-called natural law or of categorical imperatives, which make morality lifeless and rigid, a fair interpretation of what the principles of freedom and right actually are must recognize the reformative and reconstructive powers of public conscience.

In the foregoing analysis I have said repeatedly and pointedly that a declaration of liberties is also a portrait of justice. This is not a confusion of language or of categories. It is a technical point, basic for moral theory: liberty is not a mere sum of liberties. A bill of rights is not like a merchant's bill of goods; it is not a bill of particulars. Rights or liberties, in order to be genuine, must have coherence; there must be a *body* of rights or liberties, a practical compatibility among them. And this moral body is basic for the *corpus juris*. We sometimes read, especially in literature from "good old" England, about men claiming their "just liberties." This is an accurate expression, whose disuse betrays a decline of conscientiousness. There is no public liberty without justice. A liberty, like a law, must be ordered, must find its place in a system of rights. To be a right a liberty must be more than a privilege or a demand; it must be combined with a respect for the liberties of others, that is, with equity.

The wise men who wrote UNESCO's draft of a declaration of human rights, who compiled a briefer list of fifteen rights,[7] with a more critical structure than the subsequent thirty articles of the United Nations' Universal Declaration, listed as their Right No. 10 "the right to justice." This "right to justice" resembles the "right to freedom" of the Indian Constitution in being a convenient abbreviation for the conventional "civil liberties." But this is unfortunate terminology from the theoretical point of view, however convenient it may be as a practical symbol for a particular group of rights. To think of either justice or freedom as the object of a particular right leads to curious and paradoxical implications. What does it mean to have a right to righteousness? Or who would think it worth while to insist that men have a right to rights? It seems more reasonable to hold that a body of rights is well-ordered or just *as a body* when it promotes freedom, and that a body of liberties is well-ordered or right *as a whole* when it promotes justice. A system of liberties that is just can function as a norm for law; and a system of rights that promotes freedom can serve as a norm for social activities. Men are just insofar as they are careful to do what they *may* or *should* do; men are free insofar as they are careful to do what they *can* do or are *able* to do. The problem of determining either what we should do or what we can do *publicly* is solvable only when both aspects of the problem are worked out together in the context of a body of rights. In actual law, of course, there may be a big difference between what we are allowed to do and what we could do if we were allowed, but in justice and freedom the two converge, and in ideal they merge.

When the claim to liberties is overdone, when the so-called rights become so numerous or so incompatible as to reduce liberty, they cease to appear "right." When justice becomes a burden, there is something radically wrong with it; for it is fanatical to believe that justice is divine, though it makes slaves of us. Thus liberty and justice are correlatives, defining, limiting, and fortifying each other. The love of liberty prevents men from claiming too many or too pretentious rights, and the love of equity enables them to generalize, institutionalize, socialize, or make public their need for independence. If the two cease to be partners, a fanatical love of righteousness creates the conditions for the evil of oppression, and a fanatical love of liberty leads men into a chaos of collisions and frustrations. Hence justice and liberty have a common first principle: beware of making declarations of rights too long or too loose. When a man makes enemies by insisting on his rights, he should know, if he has common sense, that it is time to examine more closely his right to his claims. Rights that must be continually defended against increasing odds are suspect, for it is even harder to live by rights alone than by bread alone. One might as well be in jail as be continually in court. Hence, to know one's just liberties and to abide by them is a delicate, philosophic task.

Ralph Barton Perry, in a recent discussion of political ethics, made the following wise comment:

The ultimate value of freedom lies in what is done with it. If freedom is to be given full dignity, it must include some worthy activity, of which freedom provides the condition. . . . There is no boredom like that which can afflict people who are free, and nothing else.[8]

I might supplement this and paraphrase it by saying that the ultimate value of justice lies in what goes with it. If justice is to be given full dignity, it must include some worthy activity or form of freedom. There is no bore like the one who insists on his rights and does nothing more.

I must add in closing and also by way of summary a critical comment on "the love of the law." Liberty and justice are traditionally sacred among us; it is difficult not to learn to love them. The moral problem they raise is not the need of converting us to love them. If they appear to us in unlovable forms, we suspect that there is something wrong in the appearance, rather than in our lack of love. The primary moral problems they raise are not problems of love, but of knowledge. First, the problem of understanding how these two ideals work together to provide the basic norms of public order; secondly, the problem of knowing how to distinguish between any actual legal order and the system of rights which it is intended to serve. But in the case of law, there is a problem of love involved. Ever since the days of Moses and Plato there has been a succession of inspired reformers in our culture who have taught us to love the law. The law has been portrayed to us as something inherently perfect, delighting the soul; it is supposed to be a thoroughly rational order or self-regulating system—or, to use modern mechanical language, it is supposed to be a social mechanism with a built-in justifier. This Platonic love of the legal order has something inhuman about it; it is an achievement of a severe moral discipline. Men must be converted to it, and it is in danger of becoming fanatical and idolatrous. The great teachers who have glorified the rule of law as the reign of freedom have themselves been reformers of the law and have belied their doctrine by their example. Their love of reform has been sublimated into a vision of law idealized. Now it is evident that whether the law is lovable or not, it must be respected in order to be effective. A healthy, moral, cultivated respect for law is far from being a form of love, and far from being the love of justice and liberty. In the long run, respect for law can be maintained only by maintaining respectable laws. The law must be continually cultivated, refined. It must be decent, whether it be delightful or not. The standards by which legal decency or respectability is measured come ultimately not from the juridical order itself. They spring not from legal reason, but from the ever-living, ever-renewed, and ever-sacred love of both liberty and justice, one and inseparable.

3

EQUALITY
SECURITY
AND
PUBLIC
NEEDS

CHAPTER THREE

*Nun ist es aber so, dass das, was sich die Menschen unter
dem vorstellen, was sie brauchen, um zum Leben Ja sagen
zu können, bei jedem ein verschiedenes ist.* Das ist richtig so
und kann nicht anders sein. *Aber die Ziele des Einen können
mit denen des Anderen in Kollision geraten. Dann erfordert
es, wenn man sich nicht umbringen will, ein Sichvertragen,
einen Verzicht unter Umständen, um dem Anderen auch
sein Recht zu lassen, eine Entscheidung darüber, was wichti-
ger und was unwichtiger ist. Das Sichvertragen erfordert
also die Einsicht in eine Rangordnung der Ziele—Einsicht
in eine feste Rangordnung möglicher Zielstellungen (der
"Werte"), und das heisst, Vertrauen darauf, dass diese Rangordnung eine einsehbare ist, mit anderen Worten, es ist das*
Vertrauen auf die Vernunft. . . .

Die Angst um die Freiheit—*diese grundlegende Angst,
von der die Menschen in erster Linie befreit werden sollen—
als Angst um die Möglichkeit, sich überhaupt selbst bestim-
men zu können, ist* . . . die Angst um die Möglichkeit,
durch Einsicht in die Rangordnung möglicher Ziele in Ge-
meinschaft mit Anderen existieren zu können. *Es ist die
Angst darum, dass diese Rangordnung . . . vielleicht überhaupt keine einsehbare ist. Da eben dies heute fraglich ge-
worden ist, ist es eine* echte Angst. . . . *So konnte die Frage
entstehen ob die Erkenntnis des Menschen wirklich der* Weg
zur Wahrheit *des Seins und der Werte ist, oder ob sie nur ein*
Instrument seiner Selbstbehauptung *ist.*

Die Angst kommt also über die Menschen nicht von aussen
her, *nicht nur von den politischen Mächten, die seine Freiheit bedrohen, sondern sie hat ihren Sitz* im Zentrum des
Menschen selbst.

—LUDWIG LANDGREBE, "Freiheit Von Angst" *in*
Enquête sur la Liberté (UNESCO, 1951)

E VER since the days of Justinian Roman lawyers
have repeated the refrain taken from his Code,
"Men are born free and equal"; and ever since Cicero
orators have exclaimed that "men are by their nature
equal." These lawyers and other orators have been
well aware, as we too are aware, that men are not in
fact born equal. Some are from the start slaves,
others are masters; some are born rich, others poor;
some are naturally bright, others dull; some independent, others dependent; some healthy, others

wretched. Why, then, this traditional, insistent re-iteration of the proposition that by birth or by nature men are equal? What did those who proclaimed this doctrine really intend to say? That men have been equal? That men shall be equal? That men have a right to be equal? That men should be taken as equal? "Equal justice under law"? Or what? And we, too, when we repeat the time-honored phrase, what do we mean to say? We hesitate to say what we mean, because we know that we do not mean what we say. We know, as Justinian knew, that as a matter of fact men are not born either free or equal. We know, as Cicero knew, that human nature is not the same in all men. Then why this appeal to our status by birth or our character by nature? There are two different questions to be answered here. First, what as a matter of historical fact has been the pragmatic meaning or force of this declaration? Second, what should we now say, if we intend to be taken liter-ally?

The first question can be answered with reason-able clarity if we examine the contexts in which these declarations have been made. Under what circumstances have men asserted their equality? I believe we must agree that taken historically the doctrine of human equality is essentially negative.

It is a protest. It means in effect: no human institutions are born with man, for they are created by men. Institutions are not part of our natural environment or equipment; they are artifacts, not growths. Slavery, nobility, hereditary privileges, authority, wealth, poverty, these are not *in natura rerum* or God-given; they are cultural creations. If we are content to assert this negative doctrine, that the state of nature is not a civilized state, or that men are not by birth able to speak a language, to hold ideas, to have authority, to own property, the meaning of equality resolves itself largely into a matter of definition, not of fact. It amounts to saying that whatever social status we may have, we have socially not naturally; our social acquisitions are conventional; social distinctions come from human arrangements. Thus interpreted, the assertion of natural equality is but a restatement of the basic Greek distinction between nature and art, between growth and creation, *physis* and *poēsis*. Aristotle's talk about "natural slaves" was not intended to deny this distinction, nor need his statement that man is a political animal be interpreted to deny it. When Aristotle claimed that there are natural slaves, he did not mean to deny that slavery is a human institution; he meant only to assert that some men are incapable of self-government, which is a very different matter—a question of fact.

The classical doctrine of equality, then, has a quite negative meaning: inequalities of status or right are not natural. This does not imply in strict logic that there is such a thing as natural equality. It merely draws a sharp line between what men are by birth and what men become by convention, invention, or institution. This moralization of the meaning of status is itself one of the great achievements of civilization. Men do not naturally believe that they are born free and equal; they increasingly assert this belief as they become increasingly able to take responsibility for social inequalities.

Now, to turn to the second question, should we mean more than this by our belief in equality? Has human equality a positive content? I think it has. The belief in equality, when asserted as an article of faith, not as an opinion about birth or nature, is a more or less rhetorical way of asserting trust in equity. Equity is a positive idea and quite independent of "being born equal" or anything of the sort. Equity is a rational ideal, but it is difficult to define. To be equal and to be equitable, though in Latin they may both be covered by *aequus*, refer to two distinct relations.

Ever since Aristotle political scientists have yielded to the temptation of trying to treat equity mathematically, of reducing justice to an equation. "Equivalence" and "equilibrium" are tempting concepts for anyone who wishes to make a science of politics. It would be rewarding to survey the many ways in which minds have fallen into error by yielding to this temptation. The history of sins is not only the most entertaining of histories but also the most instructive. Suffice it to mention only two of the many forms by which equalitarian doctrine has been mathematicized, depersonalized, and eventually dehumanized, so that its intimate connection with equity and justice has been obscured. I have selected two extreme examples: the theological doctrine that all men are equal before God, because God is infinite and not a "respecter of persons," and the Benthamite doctrine that human happiness and hence human right can be measured in terms of amounts of pleasure and pain. The first rests on very primitive and popular ideas about the divine reckoning; the latter on an ultrasophisticated technique for morals and legislation; but both deny the incommensurability of human beings, and thus both assert an idea of human equivalence.

According to a very widespread and ancient ver-

sion of the Last Judgment of all men or of the ultimate, true, perfect, equitable judgment of any man,
the merit of a soul can be calculated by the balance
of good *versus* evil deeds. God's ledger is accurate
in the sense that every deed is entered in its right
place and weight in black or red, and that the worth
of the soul is determined impersonally, coolly, by
striking the balance of deeds (usually including
among deeds both actions and intentions). God,
being infinitely omniscient, does not need to be a
respecter of persons, for he is a perfect inspector of
deeds and judges a moral agent simply as the sum
of the values of his acts. Though such a theory is, of
course, not defended by theologians today, it still
operates in ecclesiastical systems of cumulative merit
and demerit and will always have a popular appeal
because of the moral simplicity and businesslike
"fairness" at its base. No judgment could be more
equitable than this of an all-seeing eye, impartial,
impersonal, keeping accurate accounts. In order to
get out from under the burden of such divine equity,
the Mahayana Buddhists and the Christians developed an equally simple, mathematical faith in infinite grace, sufficient unto all. The just judgment was
then balanced by a free mercy and a new "economy

of redemption," to use the technical Christian term, was established.

Jeremy Bentham tried to get away as far as possible from this theological calculus of merit, based on unit deeds of right and wrong. His "greatest happiness principle" was based on the psychological assumption that the effectiveness of praise and blame could be measured in terms of units of pain or pleasure, so that theoretically it should be possible to tell whether in any person's experience there was a preponderance of pain or of pleasure, and it should be possible theoretically to measure the relative strength of the preponderance. Thus, by estimating the consequences for pain and pleasure of any given act, its value for or against the "general happiness" could be determined. His dictum that the happiness of one person should be equated with the happiness of another was not so much an egalitarian moral postulate as it was a technical consequence of his impersonal calculation of amounts of pleasure and pain. It would have been more accurate to say that *whose* happiness is concerned is an irrelevant consideration. All happiness is human and can be treated as "general happiness," for the greatest happiness of the greatest number is a *social* calculation of consequences of public action in terms of *amounts* of reward or punishment. Thus Bentham worked out a secular version of the old faith in impersonal justice, units of pleasure and pain, reward and punishment, having been substituted for units of right and wrong.

Against any such attempt to reduce equity to equations or to make human beings in any literal sense equivalent to each other a truly equitable philosophy must protest. Whether it is liberalism or clericalism that makes the mistake, there is a fundamental error in all such attempts to regard human beings, or even acts, pleasures, and rights as unit values of moral measurement. This mathematical method in morals is both inhuman and abstract. A human person is indivisible and incommensurable. This is no dogmatic assumption on my part but an elementary fact of experience which no sensible person, uncontaminated by neo-Pythagorean mysticism, would care to deny. And *Gestalt* psychology has proved the point even for neo-Pythagoreans. A human being is an individual, not a unit; persons cannot be added, subtracted, or divided—only multiplied.

This elementary fact is really all that is expressed by those moralists who proclaim the "infinite worth" of each individual. The term "infinite worth" is obviously an attempt to meet the moral calculators on their own ground, but otherwise it has infinitesimal value. It is a sentimental pretense to mathematical rigor, without mathematical meaning. It has no consequences at all, and its meaning is entirely negative: it says in voluminous tones that there is no use trying to evaluate persons in scales. It follows that such phrases as "equal rights," "equal justice," and "equal consideration" are without exact meaning.

The early *Moral Economy* of Ralph Barton Perry appears to be at first glance a nonhedonistic restatement of an impersonal, calculating utilitarianism. In his "economy" any interest determines a value because it defines an aim. Hence, interests can be taken to be the ultimate subject matter of a rational ethics. Interests are the moral individuals. They should be integrated, not frustrated. A rational social order is the maximum integration of interests. All this sounds as reasonable as simple arithmetic. And as far as the present argument is concerned, I would be content to let it stand as a basis for value theory. But out of such a value theory it is impossible to construct a theory of equality or equity. An interest may be a unit value, but one interest is not equal to another. Neither Mr. Perry nor any other moralist asserts such a proposition. And Mr. Perry's subsequent writings, full of militant individualism, make it quite clear that he does not mean to use this interest theory of value as a basis for a calculus of "general happiness" either in morals or in legislation. Thus, in his *Realms of Value* (1954), though he says that "both persons and societies are organizations of interests," he also says that interests are personal and interpersonal, and his analysis of personality makes it quite clear that he does not mean to say that a person is *merely* an organization of interests or that the same kind of an organization of interests constitutes a person or a society. In short, Perry's social ethics (regardless of his value theory) is certainly closer to John Stuart Mill's concern for individuality than it is to Bentham's calculus of equity.

A tenable theory of social equality gains nothing from the attempts to treat values or interests as objective units of social measurement, for in the last analysis it is arbitrary to abstract satisfactions and fulfilments of interests from the larger complex of personal happiness and development, to which the unit values must be related. On the other hand, to bow down before every individual as an object of "infinite worth," as if all infinites were equal, is neither good mathematics nor decent ritual. Since personality is a commonplace fact, it seems sensible to accept it as an elementary datum for social theory, instead of trying to disguise it under rhetorical concepts of equality.

Now, coming to the positive point of all this polemic, and facing the individuality or indivisibility of each member of society as plain fact, we might ask, in the first place, what interest the public has in its members over and above the interest in their rights and duties. In other words, what does the idea of equality add to the idea of liberty? In what sense is equality a public concern? Or, what is the equitable aspect of equality? The only plausible answer that occurs to me is: an equitable public concern for the members is primarily a concern for the *needs* of each. When we think of "the common welfare" as the object of public interest, it is not each member's *happiness*, nor his achievements, nor the *summum bonum* that is at the center of attention; the primary object of public concern, in addition to rights, is *needs*. And, vice versa, when we as individual members ask for public support, we do so in view of our needs, not in view of our likes and dislikes; we do not ask our government to make us happy, but we think it might try to make us secure. Our need for security is basic to our other interests. Needs, like the less public interests, are intimately, inherently personal. To find out what a person needs it helps little to ask what needs he is born with; though he has native needs, his needs grow as fast as he does. On the other hand, his needs are not anything and everything that he might wish. Men's wishes and interests far exceed their needs. *Needs are what it takes to keep individuals alive as persons participating in the life of their community.* Needs are shaped by the basic conditions for personal activity. Therefore, when the early utopian socialists cried, "From each according to his capacities, to each according to his needs," they were trying to give a concrete, positive content to the doctrine of equality. To give "equal consideration" (the phrase is Tawney's) to the needs of each cannot be interpreted quantitatively; it must mean to give equitable, fair, just consideration to the needs of each. This is a much more significant and positive doctrine than the doctrine of equal rights or equal opportunities.

The chief obstacle to the acceptance of this doctrine is the fear that it is hopelessly impractical. Human needs are not only personal, they are infinitely varied. How can the public concern itself with something so intangible? The most tempting solution to this difficulty is to suppose that it is possible to discover the "natural," primary, or common needs of all—the necessities of life or the so-called animal wants of man. But this turns out to be no solution. Let me cite the classic example of Adam Smith's disillusionment on this score; he tried to base a theory of the commonwealth on "the natural wants of mankind" and quickly discovered the futility of this attempt. When Adam Smith was delivering his lectures on "public opulence," which later became his *Wealth of Nations,* he delivered a lecture entitled "Of the Natural Wants of Mankind," which ran as follows:

Nature produces for every animal everything that is sufficient to support it without having recourse to the improvement of the original production. Food, clothes and lodging are all the wants of any animal whatever, and most of the animal creation are sufficiently provided for by nature in all those wants to which their condition is liable. Such is the delicacy of man alone, that no object is produced to his liking. He finds that in everything there is need of improvement. . . . In general, however, the necessities of man are not so great but that they can be supplied by the unassisted labour of the individual. All the above necessities everyone can provide for himself, such as animals and fruits for his food, and skins for his clothing.

As the delicacy of a man's body requires much greater provision than that of any other animal, the same or rather the much greater delicacy of his mind requires a still greater provision to which all the different arts [are] subservient. Man is the only animal who is possessed of such a nicety that the very colour of an object hurts him . . .

Those qualities which are the ground of preference, and which give occasion to pleasure and pain, are the cause of many insignificant demands which we by no means stand in need of. The whole industry of human life is employed not in procuring the supply of our three humble necessities, food, clothes and lodging, but in procuring the conveniences of it according to the nicety and delicacy of our taste. To improve and multiply the materials, which are the principal objects of our necessities, gives occasion to all the variety of the arts.[1]

Thus Adam Smith began his analysis with the traditional distinction between what the human animal needs as an animal, for which he can provide "naturally" by himself, and what he humanly wants (by way of opulence) in order to satisfy the nicety and delicacy of his tastes and ideas, for which he needs division of labor and markets. But he saw at once that it was impossible to draw a sharp line between animal needs and civilized wants, for all the arts minister directly or indirectly to our need for nicety. Thus this early attempt to distinguish "productive" labor from unproductive on the ground of the satisfaction of human wants proved to be hopeless; he could not separate genuinely *public* opulence from personal delicacies and hence had no ground for a theory of commonwealth. By the time Adam Smith was ready to publish his *Wealth of Nations* he had given up this whole scheme. In the revision of his theory there is nothing about the natural wants of mankind; he substituted a single want—"man's natural tendency to barter or traffic." There is a chapter on "productive and nonproductive labor," but it is not related to a theory of needs; it deals with the accumulation of capital goods which can be exchanged. Thus, the concept of national wealth or "public opulence" gave way in his mind to the concept of capital goods or "store" of savings, which could be used as needed.

There is a double tragedy in this development of economic theory: the attempt to conceive goods in terms of the satisfaction of needs, which is morally a basic problem, was sacrificed to the theory of commodities, conceived in terms of goods for exchange; and the attempt to construct a theory of "public opulence" or commonwealth was sacrificed to the theory of capital. The so-called "welfare economists" are trying to undo this damage, but they have stumbled onto the old Utilitarian difficulty of trying to measure welfare in terms of values in general, or of human happiness. They, too, have no way of defining and delimiting needs as special objects of public concern.

I confess that to me, too, the theory of man's needs seems a hopeless task and so I am inclined to follow Adam Smith's example and drop the subject. The supposition that each individual can supply his own animal needs and thus maintain a private security as far as his physical existence is concerned is obviously absurd today, even if there were some truth in it at the time Adam Smith made the assumption. In any case, it is absurd to restrict man's basic needs to the wants which he shares with other animals. It is a tautology to say that men need the means of subsistence. They clearly need much more. The practical questions for public morals are: how much food, what kind of clothes, how good a lodging are needed in order to make the members of a community feel secure in each others' presence? To these social and psychological questions there is no universal answer. Nor is there a general answer to the still more subtle questions of social relations. How many insults will a man stand before he throws his life away to get revenge? How much oppression will he take before he sacrifices all to make a break for liberty? How much present deprivation will men accept for the sake of their future or for their posterity? What needs are more urgent than life itself? Though philosophers might try to give rational answers to these questions, the actual answers, as all students of human nature and history know, follow no rational pattern. It is practically impossible to predict either what men claim they need or what they will do when frustrated. And to decide what it is that men really need is no simpler. To declare in a grand, Schopenhauerian manner that civilization inevitably breeds discontents is too elementary an observation to merit the term "psychoanalysis"; and to indulge in an existentialist carouse on the subject of man's infinite neediness also bakes no bread except for psychoanalysts and minor prophets.

But perhaps we can make a little headway in this wilderness if we direct our attention not to the numberless needs themselves, but to the nature of a public concern for the security of citizens. Security is not one particular need among many; it is a name for the general conditions under which the satisfaction of any need can proceed. The theory of Adam Smith that this problem is solved by creating a "public store" of capital—a commonwealth of capital goods—which can be distributed by the marketing mechanisms where it is most needed has proved to be a disastrous oversimplification. Some more genuinely public and equitable mechanism is called for, one that does not rely either on a theory of natural wants or on an automatic mechanism of "fair" exchange. Is there any general, institutional provision that communities make for the security and contentment of their members which does not involve a public dictation of standardized "needs" in violation of liberty and human rights? There is one such institution that seems to me to merit particular theoretical attention, namely, insurance for social security. I am referring not to particular "social security" schemes, but to the general attempt to solve the public problem of dealing with a great variety of needs by a public system of insurance.

Let me begin this insurance theory of the commonwealth, if I may so label it, by using a few concrete illustrations. Not all men need to have their houses saved from fire, but all modern communities need public protection against loss from fire—they need fire departments and fire insurance. For if such provision were not made, those who do suffer from fire would come to the community begging for relief and the cost of the fire would be shared in some way or other. Not all men need vaccination, but all communities need a system of public health regulations, sanitation, and protection against possible plagues; for the diseased or stricken alone could not or would not pay the price. Not all men need books and those who do seldom know which book they will need next; consequently, in most communities there are public libraries, publicly supported, which try to anticipate the needs of most citizens. Such public utilities are needed not because they satisfy universal wants or common aims, but because they can anticipate possible needs of individuals. They are public means to personal needs, not common goods (in the sense that everyone needs them). They are intended to equalize the costs of contingencies or "times of need" to which all members are liable, but which will probably not be general needs. A public utility in this sense, then, may be defined as an equitable sharing in providing for possible needs, the costs of which if and when they become actual are difficult to bear personally. Such general sharing in a standard utility, though the needs which it serves may never be general, is obviously an instance of equality or equity. Mutual insurance companies, fire departments, police forces, courts, governments, may all be regarded as such public utilities, whose burdens or costs are equalized or equitably distributed, because the services they render cannot be readily or equitably marketed. Such security services supplement the price system in providing for needs. There is a clear advantage in having concrete emergency systems instead of merely a stock of capital. Public security systems of the insurance type are the counterpart of the systems of markets, for they provide unmarketable services. They should be carefully distinguished from public businesses, such as post offices, water works, power plants, toll roads and bridges, etc., the costs of which can be met by selling the product or the use of the service. Public businesses, though they are often called public utilities, are usually providers of common goods, or generally used commodities. A security service, on the other hand, is a public utility not merely because it is publicly-owned business, but because the whole community shares in providing benefits for those who especially need them, benefits which are not commodities. The network of such public services I shall call the *res publica* or commonwealth. Any community is a combination of a commonwealth and of enterprises or businesses, private or public. The security system and the commodity system supplement each other; the former is based on equality, the latter on liberty. The Tennessee Valley Authority happens to be a conspicuous example today of such

a community, in which security and business systems, equality and liberty, co-operate. But almost
any community to some degree fits this general analysis.

The general principle or obligation which binds
together members of a commonwealth is the institution of taxation, the equal or equitable apportioning
among all members of the costs of security. This
mode of equalization or equity is very commonplace indeed; but it is morally basic and should not
be overlooked. It involves the equating of costs, not
of members. It is not necessary that the members be
equal, but it is necessary that their share of the costs
be equitable. This kind of equality, this public sharing of burdens, can easily be overdone at the expense
of liberty. It would be foolish and oppressive to
provide publicly for all kinds of wants that can be
more effectively and freely satisfied by markets and
the price system. Institutions of equity should be
restricted to services which are by their nature not
commodities. If roads are used primarily by motor-
ists, and it is easy to measure the use of motor fuel, it
is obviously more just to sell the use of roads in the
form of gasoline taxes than to apportion the costs
among all members of the community. Roads can
then be paid for by the users in proportion to their

use of them, just as in the case of postal services and railroads. Whether such businesses should be administered privately or publicly is another matter, based on practical considerations. But unemployment insurance, fire departments, courts, and jails for example, could not be paid for by the consumers of the services only. The security must be by its nature collective, even though the needs are very unequal. To sum up, the two kinds of control must be balanced in the life of a well-regulated community: commonwealth and exchange, taxes and prices, equality and liberty, security through anticipating needs and satisfaction through supplying wants.

In an essay on morals it would be out of place to attempt a list or classification of the various security services which enter into a typical modern commonwealth; the aim here is to formulate moral structures, not to describe societies. However, it may serve to clarify the moral theory here suggested if we mention a few basic types of such services, and it may give a less abstract account of the *res publica*.

First, we might call attention to the system of liberties, rights, or justice, to which we have already devoted a chapter. I need not repeat here the reasons why rights are essentially public and deserve to be maintained by general taxation. How "natural" or basic our need for public justice is I shall not attempt to say. So many men and so many generations of men have devoted themselves to securing this need that it seems scarcely possible to exaggerate its importance. "More precious than life itself" is not mere rhetoric; too many have sacrificed their lives to it to permit us to regard this as an empty phrase. Self-preservation, though it is a basic animal need, seems less necessary than the "delicacy" of a public dignity and freedom.

Secondly, there is need for insurance against fear and want; men may not have a *right* to freedom from fear and want, but they certainly *need* such freedom. Absolute security is, of course, out of the question in a world full of dangers and accidents. But to provide public protection against floods, droughts, plagues, violence, and poverty, though it may not remove the causes of these evils, can at least create a more equal distribution of the pains and losses. The extension of insurance, implemented by the growth of scientific, co-operative intelligence, accounts for the most conspicuous recent developments in institutions of collective security. As these controls grow, our security and insecurity become increasingly general and both our hopes and our fears more public. The sharing of troubles provides relief to some extent, provided the troubles are not multiplied in the sharing. If our social insurance is not accompanied by social intelligence or collective prudence, the gain in equality may even entail a loss of security. For folly is a contagious disease, and there is no more terrible fear than the fear of our own police or militia. The unity created by public services creates strength but not necessarily freedom from fear. Violence is most fearful when most organized. Hence, I do not agree that we have nothing to fear but fear. Fear is at times very wholesome, especially in the presence of explosives. Without security against explosives, who would want to be free of fear?

In short, the equality created by insurance does not create responsibility. I remember once hearing Justice Brandeis say, "There is no substitute for integrity. We can protect ourselves somewhat against its absence by schemes of bonding, banking and insurance. But this game is up whenever we find it necessary to insure the insurance companies." Usually, insurance companies have a value over and above their function as equalizers, for they create capital which can be employed in the public promotion of prudence. Without such institutions of intelligence, equality not only fails to give security but also sacrifices liberty. There is truth in the old warn-

ing that equality is in danger of producing complacency, and the false security of complacency in-
creases the danger by reducing the fear. But this
warning is after all an argument against complacency, not against equality, for the two do not necessarily go together.

A third type of basic public service is protection
of individual differences. To insist on equal rights,
equal opportunities, equal consideration, and the
like is a form of fanaticism, if it means literally the
equality of conformity or sameness. The ideal of
equality is often confused with the trend toward
standardization. Individual differences are supposed
to lead to a demand for individual privileges, and
privileges to inequalities. Though it is useful for the
sake of public planning to formulate standards of
living, especially minimum standards, the use of such
concepts in statistics does not imply that standardized living has become an ideal. It is still worse when
the formula for a minimum standard becomes a general norm for "levelling downward." Such practices
are certainly a burlesque of the ideal of equality.
Neither the prophets of equality nor their disciples
have ever preached uniformity. And, especially, the
real followers of Marx, when they advocate "to each
according to his needs," would regard it as a gross

distortion of their doctrine if some dictator of the proletariat were to add, "and the Party determines your needs." Even our public needs must be actual, internally generated, not imposed on us by church or state or experts in molding public opinion. To be sure, I realize that it is impossible to draw a clear line here between genuinely personal needs and publicly inspired, standardized needs. Even in Rousseau's time, I imagine, it was practically impossible for a man to follow strictly his maxim that "each citizen must think only his own thoughts." Certainly today the arts of publicity, advertising, editorializing, and sermonizing are so highly developed and so skillfully subtle that we are none of us homemade either in mind or morals. Nevertheless, we are usually bombarded by such a variety of propaganda that we are compelled to make some choice and to exercise some independence. "To each according to his needs" is the sheerest mockery, if our institutions are not varied enough to give satisfaction to many kinds of needs. It is from this point of view especially that we must insist on the incommensurability of human beings and their happinesses. Thoreau's warning to moralists is still important, "The Golden Rule is but the best of current silver." There is no such thing as general happiness and there is no public welfare at all if it does not meet the needs of the individual citizens. Equality of opportunity, therefore, must be maintained with the emphasis on opportunities, on a wide variety of opportunities. But this is merely another way of saying that equality and liberty should develop together.

Recently I came across an attempt by a professor and statesman in Yugoslavia to state a doctrine of needs much like the one I have been defending, but in terms of Marxism. I quote a few key sentences which relate the doctrine of equality to the philosophy of law:

There are two contradictions inherent in socialism. One contrasts the rights of individual producers with the communal rights when it comes to the distribution of social products. The other treats men who are naturally and practically unequal as if they were equal when it comes to the ownership of the means of subsistence. This system of social and natural inequalities can be maintained in operation only by a *legal system*. It is this fact that makes law an inherent factor of a socialistic system. It rests on basic social relations—the relations between men and the products of their social labor. . . . All the rights of producers must be legally established in order to make them real. They must be developed and extended into a new system of democratic law. These rights presuppose the existence of enterprises that have economic and juridical individuality, and they comprise the right granted to an individual producer of appropriating a definite part of the products of social labor.[2]

Here is a clear, succinct statement of the predicament which any egalitarian government, socialistic or not, faces in trying to measure equal units of labor when laborers are unequal, to satisfy needs equally when the needs are unequal, and to give each his share, though the commonwealth itself must take a share. Some legal system of equity is necessary to give equality concrete meaning and effect so long as producers and consumers vary in capacities, interests, and needs. This explanation that even Marxian socialism needs a legal system and a set of rights also implies that no legal system can pretend to be equitable unless it takes into account the needs of individuals and the costs of the commonwealth.

Lastly, I mention one more type of public service in meeting personal needs—institutions of public education. By public education I mean more than a system of public schools. We can demand public schools as a right, but we need more. We need to let our interests interact publicly and instructively, so that in pursuing one interest after another we gradually learn how to avoid an endless series of distractions and frustrations and can effectively engage in something that may be called a real pursuit of happiness. We may not actually need happiness, but we certainly need to pursue it. And such a pursuit implies a process of learning about the interrelations of our own needs, about the relations of our needs to those of our fellow-citizens, and about the relations of our needs, our fellows' needs, and the needs of other communities to our commonwealth's needs. Doing what we please will not get us what we want, and even after we know what we want we must still learn what we need. Hence, the knowledge of needs is the basic discipline of public education. And yet there is no professor in any department of any university who can teach it. This knowledge is difficult to professionalize and impossible to summarize. Karl Marx tried to summarize it by proclaiming that the annihilation of classes is our basic need, and that this annihilation implies substituting for the "bourgeois" doctrine of equal rights the gospel of "equal obligations for all." [3] But we have already seen that obligations are just as varied as rights, and no more democratic. Neither the abolition of classes nor the equating of obligations is a positive solution to the problem of determining our needs, for the basic problem is not a problem of "annihilation" at all. No amount of social "levelling," to use the seventeenth-century term, will throw much light on human needs. The real problem is a problem of *adaequatio,* to use the medieval term, that is, of discovering specific compatibilities and adjustments. And this is a personal problem.

Other moral scientists insist that the knowledge of needs depends on the knowledge of an objective scale of values. I do not wish to deny that a problem of values is involved in the knowledge of needs, and that an *adaequatio* or co-ordination of needs is related to scales of value. But I do not follow Professor Landgrebe's argument (in the passage cited at the beginning of this chapter) when he claims that the knowledge of what we need for public purposes is dependent on the discovery of a scale of possible aims (*Rangordnung möglicher Ziele*). Admitting that the science of the compatibility of *aims* may be a problem of *rational* discipline or theoretical intelligence (*ein Vertrauen auf die Vernunft*), though I believe this is admitting too much, the knowledge of the compatibility of *needs* is a distinct and essentially *social* discipline in *public* adjustments, and this knowledge is based not on a general insight into the order of all *possible* aims but on a continual contact with actual social conditions. This is a social art rather than a theoretical science. Here Adam Smith's observation seems to me straight to the point, when he argued that for the satisfaction even of our basic needs it takes all the arts, the sciences, and the virtues. Gradually in social experience we learn that we may not need now what we used to need, or that we may not need at all what we think we need, and we arrive at the difficult art of developing good taste and character by the process of tempering our actual desires to our probable needs, rather than tempering our possible needs to our actual desires. This science of public manners and good judgment, if it be a science, is even more basic to the pursuit of happiness than the science of so-called rational aims. Our personal needs must be determined in the context of our public resources. We are apt to measure our resources in terms of our purchasing power, and our purchasing power in terms of what someone who has something to sell thinks we ought to be able to afford. Under these circumstances is it flattering and stimulating to let others tell us what we need, but it is also corrupting. There is no intelligent pursuit of happiness where there is not at least an attempt at moral self-government. Such self-government is not moral isolationism. On the contrary, it is the art of making a responsible appropriation of public resources, budgeting our needs as members of a commonwealth. Whether this art be called the pursuit of happiness or the discipline of good taste is a minor matter of rhetoric; the essential matter is the democratization of personal freedom and moral judgment. There is no adequate ethics for public life where there is no public recognition of this responsibility on the part of all citizens. To be a decent citizen a person must be able to adapt his needs to his resources and to measure both his needs and his resources in terms of the commonwealth. John Erskine once wrote an essay on "the moral obligation to be intelligent." It is precisely this obligation that needs to be recognized. An obligation is recognized, however, not when it is preached, but when it is understood; and this particular obligation suffers, I think, from being over-preached and under-clarified. In any society where the great majority of members are deprived of the basic means of information, of critical judgment, and of self-knowledge, there cannot be freedom from fear and there will not be freedom from want; security must then be imposed by authority and moral judgment by social hierarchy. Neither equality nor liberty then have a chance.

Some students of politics still regard all this as merely a revolutionary faith, and more regard it still as visionary. Too many of us pay only lip service to it. But as our political experience and our public needs grow we are compelled to take it more seriously as a reflective and positive judgment. For these doctrines of the Enlightenment are still proving to be truly enlightened.

4
FRATERNITY
CHARITY
AND
CIVIC
VIRTUES

Fraternity, liberty and equality isolated from communal life are hopeless abstractions. Their separate assertion leads to mushy sentimentalism or else to extravagant and fanatical violence which in the end defeats its own aims. Equality then becomes a creed of mechanical identity which is false to facts and impossible of realization. . . . Liberty is then thought of as independence of social ties, and ends in dissolution and anarchy. It is more difficult to sever the idea of brotherhood from that of a community, and hence it is either practically ignored in the movements which identify democracy with Individualism, or else it is a sentimentally appended tag. In its just connection with communal experience, fraternity is another name for the consciously appreciated goods which accrue from an association in which all share, and which give direction to the conduct of each. . . .

It is said, and said truly, that for the world's peace it is necessary that we understand the peoples of foreign lands. How well do we understand, I wonder, our next door neighbors? It has also been said that if a man love not his fellow man whom he has seen, he cannot love the God whom he has not seen. The chances of regard for distant peoples being effective as long as there is no close neighborhood experience to bring with it insight and understanding of neighbors do not seem better. A man who has not been seen in the daily relations of life may inspire admiration, emulation, servile subjection, fanatical partisanship, hero worship; but not love and understanding, save as they radiate from the attachments of a near-by union. Democracy must begin at home, and its home is the neighborly community.

—JOHN DEWEY, The Public and Its Problems, *by permission of the publishers, Henry Holt & Company*

Public life is three-dimensional: it makes certain demands, it ministers to certain needs, and it cultivates certain personal standards. The demands which members of a community make on each other establish a social framework, structure, or constitution, which is too often interpreted as the very substance or foundation of a society. It is really society's skeleton. The constitutional system of rights and duties is what Aristotelians call the "formal cause," the shape or pattern of a society. Public needs, on the other hand, determine the objectives, services, or "final causes" of communal living. Civic virtues are the "efficient cause," the energy or working power which keeps the whole structure going. Fraternity, in other words, is what it takes to give a community vitality.

Virtues of any sort are not popular among up-to-date moralists; when conspicuous they spoil society, much as a parade interrupts normal traffic. They are a sour, moldy, overripe, disagreeable subject of conversation, though they may be preached privately, discreetly, to children. In college studies they may occasionally appear in the texts of required courses, but the less said about them the better. And civic virtue or public spirit, despite its honorable career from Cicero to Montesquieu, evokes scornful smiles. Psychologists tell us it is an exploded myth and politicians no longer count on it. I can recall how, back in 1919, when New Yorkers were enjoying the double democracy of Woodrow Wilson and Tammany Hall, the Woodrow Wilson faction thought it would be a noble gesture to put a statue of civic virtue on Park Row between the statue of Horace Greeley and City Hall. They found in MacMonnies a competent sculptor, who composed a "colossal group" out of shining white marble upon which New Yorkers could gaze on their way to work from Brooklyn Bridge to Wall Street. There was a Tarzan-like youth standing on some shells, if I remember correctly, very erect and innocent, carrying a broken sword, and looking intently at the steeple of St. Paul's Chapel, while about his ankles and knees there swam and sported a few very tempting sirens, mermaids, or some such fish. After a few years of this exposure in City Hall Park, during which time the statue had become an all too eloquent symbol for satire on the public morals of New York, the city fathers took pity on us and removed "Civic Virtue" to somewhere near the Zoo. It would be distasteful to me, if I had to end this analysis of public morality with a sermon on civic virtue, and therefore I am grateful to the framers of the French Revolution for having changed the popular terminology to "fraternity." Unfortunately, this term, too, has lost much of its popularity in the course of a century of abuse, and I may have trouble in making it seem not only respectable but vital.

What is fraternity and wherein lies its virtue? I must begin my reply cautiously by explaining what fraternity is not. Aristotle in his portrait of the idea of a Greek political community interpreted the bond of fellow citizenship as a development of friendship (*philia*). *"Philadelphia"* or "brotherly love" has been reasserted religiously and convincingly in modern times by the Quakers as the basis of both citizenship and religious communion. But does modern public life imply a society of friends? This question must be taken seriously in view of the impressive history which the ideal has enjoyed. It seems fantastic, however, under modern living conditions to believe that fellow citizens must be friends. By most of us today friendship is taken to be a private relation, an intimate and emotional bond. Admitting that Aristotle may have described accurately a practical ideal for the Greek city-state, and admitting that his analysis of friendship is still a true picture of what it has always meant to be friends, it seems impossible that citizens today can be expected to have as much in common and to be as closely united as friends are. There is a distinct separation, at least in a typical modern city though perhaps not in a village, between our personal relations and our public relations. Our friends need not be our neighbors and our neighbors need not be our friends. We can be business partners, fellow-employees, members of the same political party, company, team, college class, labor union, church, without being friends in the full, Aristotelian sense of the term. Friendship is certainly a form of love, but is brotherhood a form of love? I have been studying both brothers and fraternities for a long time, with this question in mind, and am convinced that "love" is not the proper word to use in this connection. I am not denying that brothers may be and may well be friends, loving one another, but the essential thing about the fraternal relation is not that. What is essential to brothers is that they must learn to live together. They must know how to put up with each other, to be close and yet in peace. And they must help each other when there is danger or trouble.

Now, there is a definite similarity between this discipline of being brotherly and civic virtue. Even though in public fellow-citizens need not feel any personal ties which make them desire to be together, they must keep the peace, must deal respectfully with each other, be decent, whether they feel like it or not. If, then, we interpret brotherhood not as a form of love but as a moral discipline, there is certainly a real point in preaching fraternity to fellow-citizens. But it is not correct to imply that the public or civic relation needs the same personal intimacy and reciprocal concern that private brotherhood entails. Fraternities or other groups of friends when they take on organized form are more apt to become clubs or religious communions than public associations. Clubs and religious fellowships are notoriously poor models for civic fraternity.

There is a second trait in the classic idea of community that is supposed to be essential to civic virtue, namely, devotion to the general welfare or group interest. Each citizen is supposed to be virtuous insofar as he has two wills—a particular will and a "general will," an interest of his own and a public interest. To be public-spirited is said to be an eminent and difficult virtue, according to this theory. Montesquieu, Rousseau, and Jefferson, to say nothing of Cicero and the more ancient preachers of this public spirit, analyzed in considerable detail both the necessity and the difficulty of this virtue. To them it represented true nobility, for they believed firmly that no republic could endure unless its citizens were endowed with a rare, distinctive ability to sacrifice personal interests and to be what Plato called the "guardians" of the universal good. Idealists have persistently reasserted this doctrine that there can be no genuine community without a common good, and no common good without a general will. Nevertheless, it is common knowledge that it is assuming too much even of brothers to believe that they must have at bottom a common life and common aims. Com-

munism of values is an even more extravagant demand to make on one's fellow-citizens than communism of property. Is it really necessary that we be
literally comrades, partners, co-workers to be fellow-
citizens? No doubt a community is more solid and
morally simple if there is such a unity of purpose.
But is this unity of purpose essential? Is a neighborhood necessarily like a team or a factory or an army,
integrated by its interests?

Insofar as the classical concept of "republican
virtue" is supplanted by the concept of "fraternity,"
there is at least an implicit recognition that the classical concept had asked for too much. Citizens, like
brothers, may not agree in their aims and may differ
considerably even in their basic ideals, but they
nevertheless learn to practice self-restraint, decent
manners, public respectfulness toward each other,
and to agree to a certain amount of sharing. The real
reason why civic virtue is difficult to acquire has little
to do with the difficulty of agreeing on a common
good, but much to do with the habit of treating po-
litely and decently, without hypocrisy, in our public
relations those whom privately we do not respect.
Among neighbors it is necessary to keep self-respect
and yet to be decent and equitable toward those who
are not friends, or comrades, or co-workers, or even

trustworthy customers. There are limits, of course, for any virtue is subject to strain beyond endurance and justice is doubly strained. But within limits fellow-citizens must learn the art of forbearance and the willingness to live with those whose views and values they do not share. Friendship is no adequate basis for public relations.

Now, having distinguished the public virtues from others, having explained what fraternity is not, I must try to outline fraternity's positive content. My general thesis is that community spirit, not being a unity of aims or values, is a unity of rights, duties, and needs. The general welfare, as it is commonly called, is not a general happiness nor a common good but a willingness in all to share enough to provide for the rights and needs of each.

The minimum of fraternity is charitableness. Charity is more than toleration. Toleration may be merely, to use a Roman Catholic definition, "patience with evil." Charity implies a more positive social bond— a slowness to anger, a refraining from public judgment, an awareness of human fallibility and folly, and a positive effort to understand and sympathize. Sympathy should not be conceived as an emotional state but rather as an intellectual and moral discipline, in virtue of which a neighbor tries to find some positive ground for meeting and sharing with his neighbor, though he thinks him to be benighted, vulgar, or even vicious. Neighbors who can meet on the ground of a common *faith* have a fairly easy time of it. To be a member of a political party or of a religious communion is a very different kind of membership from membership in a community, which must embrace a variety of parties and religions. Charity must transcend unity of faith. In communities where solidarity of faith is absent, there is a tendency of the members to fall back on *hope*. Unity may still come about, they hope, when the others discover the error of their ways and are prepared to embrace the truth. It would be a hard life indeed for modern fellow-citizens who find themselves in opposing party lines to be forced to conclude that their party lines are everlasting and that no reconciliation or no new basis of common accord is possible. We are becoming accustomed to the idea that party politics is essential to democratic communities, and yet we condemn partisanship, factionalism, and hopeless irreconcilables. We implicitly expect that the forces which divide our political communities may someday give way to hidden grounds of unity. We mingle disgust with hope, even when we fail to understand a ground for hope. For even a blind hope has a vestige of faith in it. Such faith and such hope, stronger than faith, are important public goods, to be sure, but "the greatest of these is *charity*." All is not lost in a community when a common faith and mutual hope fade, provided there remains a spirit of charitableness. This is the basic minimum of sociability. And it has great powers of endurance because it seeks to understand; it is an intellectual virtue as well as a social one. To agree to disagree is still a form of agreement and may provide a positive ground for community.

Even those who inflict suffering on each other may discover in their "community of suffering" a basis for charity—not a very positive basis, to be sure, but still a possible, tragic dignity as among "honorable enemies." There is a significant difference between an ordinary brawl and a formal contention. There is a moving passage in Dante's *Monarchia* where he describes those contenders who meet each other "under God," not in anger but out of zeal for the vindication of truth, and he adds that armies are not worthy of the "prize" of world power if they fail to meet "under God," that is, for love of justice. Such attempts to find community even in warfare may appear to modern minds as straining morality to a grotesque extreme or as sanctifying a "church militant" version of society. And yet there is in most modern communities an element of organized struggle embedded in the very structure and quality of public life. To regard a typical modern community as a "harmony" is the most grotesque misunderstanding. Fraternity is seldom solidarity; and today, as one looks at the world, the most conspicuous type of fraternity is a contentious, grudging type of charity, which could scarcely bear the name of neighborliness.

But even when torn by conflicts, a community may exhibit something more than bare charity, something less than neighborliness; in between these two virtues there is a kind of dogged conscientiousness, a formal public decency based on sheer respect for the rights and needs of the members. When the personal relations or class interests among citizens become embittered, so that it would not be true to say that as persons the members of the community care for each other, they may nevertheless respect liberty and equality as institutions. Here charity is supplemented by a fraternal agreement to maintain the institutions of freedom and equity even though there may be agreement on nothing else; this negative kind of fraternity amounts to little more than a renunciation of violence in class struggle or political rivalry. Of course, no one would call such a community happy or healthy, and no one would give it long to live. For in the long run man cannot live by virtue alone, and fraternity is desperate if it has nothing but liberty and equality to live for. This whole moral order is not worth maintaining, if it serves no other interests and brings happiness to no one. Public decency itself is indecent when it cloaks a rotting society. Men must enjoy living together, otherwise their loyalty to the institutions of democracy is a hollow righteousness and vanity. Hence brotherhood must be more than a bare public virtue, to be genuinely social; it must be also an expression of man's social nature.

On the other hand, fraternity, if it tries to get along by itself, relying on man's social instincts rather than on a respect for the rights and needs of men, generates the worst forms of fanaticism and tyranny. Josiah Royce used to argue that loyalty is an absolute virtue, an end in itself, the more of it the better. But our generation has seen enough of fanatic fraternity to realize that loyalty, like other virtues, must be tempered, sobered, so that it performs a reasonable service for other interests.

Fraternity, therefore, is not a complete virtue until the charity and decency on which it depends yield a genuine neighborliness. A neighborhood is usually defined in terms of a local, face-to-face community, whose members, being obliged to live in physical proximity, must learn to share some of their interests, services, and standards sufficiently to give the community a physical stability and agreeableness. But ever since the question was raised, "Who is my neighbor?" there has been a growing realization that a neighborhood should not be conceived too spatially and locally. In the complicated structure of modern urban life and of national and international communities it is especially important to conceive public relations not so much geographically as institutionally or functionally. In other words, the members of a professional group, though widely scattered, may get together often enough to "keep in touch" with each other, and they then constitute a real community as well as an organization for the promotion of certain interests. It remains true that a neighborhood implies a cultivation of personal bonds, direct communication, sharing of interests, diversity of interests, and sympathy, which is more than belonging to a businesslike corporation or holding a membership card in an "association." But with modern means of communication such neighborly relations need not be confined to villages or towns or even nations. On the contrary, it is possible now to develop freer, more agreeable, and meaningful types of neighborly bonds than the traditional local neighborhood provided.

One such form of fraternity, which transcends local neighborliness, is the conscious and active "belonging" to a people, the sharing in a particular culture. A culture "area" is really more temporal than spatial. Whether national or not, it usually unites into a fellowship all who share or have shared a common language, common victories, common defeats, a common heritage of literature and other arts, and who feel themselves drawn together in the promotion of their common arts and faiths, or perhaps more negatively in fear of other peoples or in competition with other cultures. To belong to a people or a culture in this sense is more than a matter of physical inheritance, more than a social heritage, and more than a national loyalty. A people need not be a state or a nation, but it must have a strong historical dimension; it is a continuity of generations—a continuity that does not depend necessarily on blood or soil, but that comes from the cumulative sharing by one generation in the work of others. It is a tradition plus the making and breaking of traditions. A people is a brotherhood insofar as its members can participate directly and meaningfully in the cultural heritage. Without the general right and the particular means of participation the community is broken; and without a lively communication between the present gen-

eration and those of the past and future a cultural
community loses its distinctive power and appeal.
Modern means of education, art, and enjoyment have
made the temporal extension of our cultures no less
spectacular than the spatial extension. In short, men
can now find their neighbors in the most unexpected
times and places, so that it is difficult to identify and
locate communities. And this is true of cultures, too;
more peoples and more generations can now live together than ever before.

As the community of a people transcends the life
of any of its generations in time, so, as peoples become neighborly, there are gradually forming communities of peoples which transcend the territorial
limits of any one people. They are sometimes called
"families of nations," but the more accurate and
technical term for these intercultural neighborhoods
is "federal unions." I do not mean here the political
aspects of federal organization, and the technicali-
ties of co-ordinate authority, for I wish here to
show that even non-political federations of peoples
involve new and distinctive forms of moral structure.

The United States were originally conceived as
such a federation of peoples, and as late as Calhoun
there were political philosophers who still insisted

that there is no such thing as "we, the people of the United States." This radical, federal interpretation of the community of the United States is now generally regarded as a legal fiction, for there obviously is a single national community now, which is taking its place in the "family of nations." Nevertheless, this people, though it is more than a federation, is in a peculiar degree an international people. It is not only a mixture of all the European peoples and cultures, but it now contains many important elements of Asian and African cultures. Thus the culture of the United States is a uniquely complicated one. From the European point of view it represents an experiment in European neighborliness, an experiment which many Europeans still view with alarm! American culture is being used extensively in Europe today as an argument both pro and con a European neighborhood on European territory. But this raises the question of the fruitfulness of cultural mixtures; cultural federations are a different kind of experiment.

There are several genuine international federal communities which are not mere alliances of states but neighborhoods of peoples. The Organization of American States, recently created, would probably be regarded as little more than an institutional expression of a "good neighbor policy" in politics and economics. However, it is still in its infancy and might become the organ of a Pan-American federal neighborhood. Such a neighborhood of American peoples now seems a rather remote possibility because of the relatively few cultural ties that unite North and South America, compared with the strong bonds that tie each of the American continents to Europe. In fact, here is a good illustration of the prevalence of historical over spatial or geographical factors in forming cultural unions. A more promising neighborhood is Europe, which is actively groping for a cultural federation of peoples as a moral necessity, over and above the question of a military or political federation. Europe has long been more than a geographical expression and is now conscious of strong reasons why it must seek to become a genuine neighborhood. The British Commonwealth of Nations is a federal community in which the political structure is increasingly yielding to cultural bonds. The U.S.S.R., erroneously known as Russia, is supposed to be a federation of peoples. Then there is the Arab League, which is already more than a political expedient. And an intercultural neighborhood seems to be forming in southeast Asia. Such federations have an immediate political function and origin, but, being based also on geographical "culture areas," they may well become fraternal communities in a broader, moral sense. Such fraternal federations put a special emphasis on equality, since the members are supposed to treat each other as sovereign states. However, in most of these systems there is about as much equality as there is in the solar system between the sun and its planets. In general, the concept of international equality is at least as vague as that of individual equality. But here, as in the relations among individuals, the theory of equality really means that the members of the federation are concerned fraternally for the needs of each sovereign member. How far such groupings of peoples with common needs may go toward developing international neighborhoods remains to be seen, but it is already clear that the concept of fraternity has practical international application.

It has been a traditional dogma of Roman law that whatever is necessary to the welfare of the people has the highest legal sanction: *salus populi suprema lex.* And this maxim has been interpreted to mean that a government should look out for the welfare *only* of its own subjects. I remember with what earnestness a young Italian Fascist once, at the time of the Ethiopian crisis, praised the British Government to me: "There," he said, "is the best government in the world, for it consistently and intelligently looks after the interests of the British people." This ancient doctrine, that a sovereign government is ultimately responsible only for the welfare of its subjects, has been generally respected as the last word in political morals. And it seems a hard doctrine indeed to a practical politician that a government should be expected to adjust the welfare of its own people to that of neighboring peoples; he would sooner believe that intergovernmental friendships are out of the question *in principle*. And yet a recognition of such an international obligation to be neighborly is now being forced on almost all governments. The old argument is that it is only insofar as our own peace and prosperity depend in part on the peace and prosperity of other peoples that our government has any interest or obligation to help others. But putting the international obligations thus on a mere basis of prudence or business is no longer adequate to meet the needs of the international communities that are forming rapidly. The positive doctrine of international fraternity as a public virtue and duty is therefore rapidly gaining ground. "Most-favored-nation" is no longer an adequate ideological ground for foreign trade treaties; and "good neighbor policy" is taking on a more concrete significance and practical reality. Similarly, the old mercantilist ideal of each nation maintaining a favorable balance of trade, though it still has its use in calculating relative credit, is being supplemented by less orthodox economic policies. International credits, gifts, alliances, cartels, pools, etc., are all symptoms of an increasing international business community, which must inevitably lead to a wider international neighborhood.

The culminating attempt at the creation of a federal community of peoples is, of course, the United Nations and its affiliated specialized agencies. These member nations are, to be sure, not really united, and they are as yet further from being a genuine federal community than some of the more restricted neighborhoods of peoples which we have just mentioned. There may even be a serious competition between the international neighborhoods and the United Nations; for strong cultural ties usually outpull the more political unions in the long run, and to build out of the political mechanisms of the United Nations a genuine cultural community on a worldwide scale will take time. In the meantime the various "culture area" neighborhoods may have become exclusive fraternities. A world community is an idea to which we have long paid theoretical tribute, but the practical cultivation of neighborly virtues on such a scale requires the invention of appropriate institutional machinery. A community cannot live without communication. Already revolutionary progress has been made in world-wide communication through press, radio, travel, education, personal exchanges, treaties, and associations of all sorts. This revolution must go still further in providing the necessary community tools. We must become reconciled to a revolution in social machinery analogous to the industrial revolution. For it is only through a continual increase in the variety and directness of personal contacts across cultural lines, only through an actual becoming acquainted on a world-wide scale, that world community can become a reality. And just because it is visionary and foolish to expect the whole world to become acquainted immediately, we must be on our guard against expecting too much from the so-called "Great Community." After all, it was world war that brought the world together in conflict; it would be a miracle if the contacts of fighting could be transformed into bonds of fraternity without the many means of communication and service by which local communities keep alive.

In the above analysis I have taken the international approach to world community, trying to understand how communities can be compounded or federated into more inclusive communities, until ideally all peoples are neighbors really. But there is another approach to the idea of human brotherhood, which is a big short cut. This is the religious approach, based on the idea that all men under God are inherently a family and owe each other fraternal respect and regard. This religious faith in the City of God is, strictly speaking, outside the scope of a treatise on public morality. It makes its appeal to men intimately through religious fellowship. Nevertheless, we cannot afford to ignore it, since religious communions take on public forms and responsibilities. There are at least three classic variations of this idea, which deserve to be considered separately. I shall not attempt to discuss them historically, since all three have had ancient origins and long careers.

(1) The first approach is the belief in human social unity on the ground of the unity of creation. "God hath made of one blood all nations." Or, to use modern biological language, men are a single species related by inheritance, and related ultimately to the whole world of living beings. This extension of the idea of fatherhood and of family ties to all mankind is essentially a religious development of the

ethics of kinship. It is tribalism to the nth degree; infinite clannishness. Now, it is true that when clannishness becomes all-inclusive it loses one of its obnoxious features. Still, the appeal to blood unity or to solidarity by origin is hardly compatible with a civic or civil conception of fraternity. The ancient Greeks and Hebrews and the modern Europeans experienced the crises created by the conflict between tribal and civic loyalties. Hence, to appeal to the unity of mankind on the ground of a unity of creation is, after all, not an appeal to a community in a public sense. It is an attempt to extend the love that unites families to include all men. Religiously this idea is intelligible and important, but morally it is impossible to universalize a family without destroying its distinctive features, bonds, and virtues. When families become as large as clans they lose most of their virtues, and when all men love a common father, they may still be very far from constituting a universal brotherhood. Rather, each child of God has an intimate, private bond to an infinitely loving father. Much religion is an extension of parental relations, whether it is infantilism, as some claim, or not; it is psychologically superficial to expect this religious extension of bonds between parent and child to carry with it a sense of religious fraternity.

The two emotions are quite distinct. Religious fraternities and fellowships are often genuine families, practicing fraternal virtues and glorifying them by worshipping a heavenly father; but such fellowships are socially exclusive and are religiously valuable because they are exclusive. A religious fellowship that strives to embrace all mankind generates a large number of orders, distinctive fellowships, and sects, by means of which it continues to have the vitality of "being not of the world" and of being a particular religion at the same time that it professes to be a universal brotherhood in ideal. Neither is religious fellowship dependent on the doctrine of the unity of creation, nor is the belief in the unity of creation necessarily a basis for fellowship.

(2) A second form of the ideal of a universal fraternity is the Stoic ideal of cosmopolitanism. This is clearly an extension of the civic community to include all men and the whole universe under the single rule of Divine Reason. The more popular idea of God as "King of the Universe" did not imply cosmopolitanism. It was the Stoic universalization of the city-state idea that created the idea of world citizenship, an idea which was in striking contrast to the early Christian belief that Christians are "citizens of Heaven," not of this world. The appeal to universal

citizenship depends for its power on one's faith in natural moral law. This faith has certainly persisted to our own day, having been revived in our own generation after it had undergone almost two centuries of attack; and wherever it is held, wherever the universe is still believed to be a moral cosmos, men will appeal to it as an absolute ground for a universal community and as an absolute ground for condemning man's actual politics. Such cosmopolitanism makes an admirable ground for public morality as well as for natural religion. The chief trouble with the ideal is that modern views of the physical universe have undermined much of the ancient idea that the astronomical framework has something to do with the moral order. It is now very difficult to conceive a cosmos, that is, a universal rule of reason which both men and stars obey. However, it is possible to detach cosmopolitanism from the belief in a cosmos and to make it merely a kind of humanism with a halo. But without the cosmos orientation the faith loses much of its religious power; and as a gospel for a universal humanitarianism, its value as a practical ideal depends largely on the growth of the Great Community which it heralds.

(3) The third religious form of faith in universal brotherhood is based on the idea of the divine judg-

ment, all men being equal in the sight and love of
God. I have already examined one aspect of this concept in connection with the discussion of the idea of
equality, and I need not repeat here what I said then
about the difference between man's relation to God's
judgment and men's relations to each other. This
faith can be asserted, and usually is asserted, independently of man's public communities. It is an in-
vitation to a universal communion regardless of wars
and sects. But there is little direct relation between
such public communions with the just and perfect
judge, except by way of contrast with human judgment, and men's other public fraternities. For when
men of one or many communions or communities
assemble in public worship, each is supposed to humble himself before God in unconditional surrender to
justice. Each communicant alone, though in public,
faces the divine judgment and mercy. But when
these communicants then turn, after worship, and
face each other, they are in a totally different set of
relations and their social and moral bonds take the
place of their "equality" before God. In other words,
if religious communion is conceived not as a bond
between man and God but as a bond between man
and man and God, as members of the Kingdom of
God, the idea of communion is bound to become

ecclesiastical and hence loses the universal values inherent in the idea of the divine judgment, for no ecclesiastical community is universal for mankind. Thus this popular notion of all men being under the government of God is apt to confuse three distinct things: communion with God, church communions or religious fellowships, and public communities or congregations as community institutions. In this state of affairs it would be pedantic to insist on a clear separation between civic morality and religion; the two are intertwined in theory and practice. Directly or indirectly men in their daily social relations will be influenced by their relations to God in worship and to fellow church members on holy days. But, admitting this fact, we cannot infer that, since all men appear before God for just and merciful judgments, they will also appear before each other as brothers in justice and mercy. On the contrary, the communities that are often the most difficult to persuade to join a universal brotherhood are those which have their own particular way of proclaiming the divine fatherhood. A universal religious fellowship would certainly be impractical without more general cultural unity, for the popular strength of religious communities lies in their ties with local cultures rather than in the universality of their gospel. It is therefore quite intelligible that while each religious fellowship preaches the brotherhood of all mankind they cannot practice much fraternity among themselves. Nevertheless, there are many signs at present that religious leaders are becoming more respectful of each other and that there is an increasing "ecumenical" ideal, according to which religions are cooperative in bringing charity and peace on earth even when their ways of salvation are competitive. If the religions of mankind should become genuinely charitable toward each other, this event would certainly mark a most important step toward a secular fraternity among nations.

EPILOGUE

THE foregoing analysis of liberty, equality, and fraternity in terms of the dimensions of public morality has been dominated by two considerations: first, the attempt to show the essential interrelatedness of these three dimensions and thus to explain why the isolation of any one from the three-dimensional continuum of public life produces abstractions in theory and abominations in practice; and secondly, the attempt to conceive public affairs in the broadest possible sense as the concerns of whatever communities man has built, from the most local to the world-wide, and from the relatively private to the most public. Consequently I may have portrayed *res publica* in too Ciceronian a rhetoric, and may have failed to suggest the implications of the analysis for any particular community. In avoiding the temptation to narrow public affairs to the business or art of politics and statecraft, I did not mean to fall into the opposite extreme of glorifying *res publica* in Stoic fashion, hailing it as "dear City of God." I have intentionally left the term "public" vague, though I have used *"res publica"* or "commonwealth" technically for something concrete. My statements have been generalities, but, I trust, not abstractions.

Before I close this elementary treatise in moral philosophy I might try to make amends for this very general treatment of my subject by applying the analysis to a particular case, to a familiar community whose three dimensions have often been discussed. Hence, instead of recalling at the end the big, black, three-cornered world public, with which I began, let me now call attention to the three branches of the Federal Government of the United States. I say "branches" rather than "powers," because I wish to presuppose the single, living trunk of the commonwealth, which unites and empowers the branches, and which, in turn, is rooted in the people or community of the United States. There is a classical tradition, which still has its devotees, according to which a government is and should be composed of three separate powers. Each power, they say, has its own distinctive weapons, energies, and virtues; each has an eye on the other two; and together they constitute a system of checks and balances which is the guardian of our liberties and which keeps the commonwealth in equilibrium. How does our analysis bear on this doctrine of the separation of powers?

There is more than a verbal difference between "separation of powers" and "distinction of dimensions." Powers are intelligible separately and are supposed to operate independently; dimensions are necessarily correlatives, aspects of a single body. Let me suppose, in order to simplify the diagram, that the judicial branch is the chief protector of our liberties and rights, that the executive branch has the task of providing for our needs and security, and that the legislative branch is kept busy cultivating fraternity among a number of competing interests, "warring factions" (as they were originally called), or "public parties" (to use a more dignified name for them). This ought to pass as a rough, but realistic, classification of the chief functions of the three branches in terms of liberty, equality, and fraternity. Put in this way, the three branches represent not a separation of powers but a division of labor. Division of labor implies, first of all, labor. It is well to think of public officials as doing public work, not as merely "holding office" or "exercising" authority. The work of government, in other words, is productive labor, not as Adam Smith used to teach and as the Marxists still teach, *outside* the system of production. These three types of officials do different kinds of work, perform distinct services. The division of labor, furthermore, implies an exchanging or sharing of the products of these diversified, specialized departments of the commonwealth. Division of labor implies a positive correlation, co-ordination of goods and services produced, which is more than a mere checking and balancing process. When a judge defines a right, an undersecretary administers a public utility, or a congressman proposes a bill for majority approval, these officials are not engaged in checking and balancing each other. At least, they ought not so to construe their offices. They are each performing a specialized task for the commonwealth, and as a result of this work the rights, needs, and virtues of the members of the commonwealth are clarified and correlated,

The public concerns of each citizen are reflected in the types of public labor performed by the officials. Public affairs are more than official affairs; not only the "authority" but every authorizing citizen is in and of the public. Human beings in their private lives have other concerns and live in still more dimensions, but insofar as they are concerned about their rights, their needs, and their civic virtues they call upon the help of professional specialists in these matters to solve their problems.

It is because the souls of citizens, if I may revert to the language and analysis of Plato's *Republic,* have this three-dimensional moral structure that the commonwealth is composed of "classes." It is not the existence of a class of guardians that gives rise to special privileges and duties; it is the existence of a need for security in each soul that gives rise to the class of guardians. A well-classified public is one which accurately reflects the public dimensions of a well-developed soul. Hence, as Plato tried to tell us, the *res publica* is *within* us. And in each soul, each commonwealth, these public concerns must be adjusted not only to each other but to the private concerns which make us persons. In this sense, it may be true enough to say that each citizen in his triple relationship with his government must learn the art of checking and balancing his rights, needs, and civic virtues; but this is merely another way of referring to moral discipline in general.

I have used the old language of republican trinitarianism. The doctrine of three-in-one is as important for society as it is for theology. But I do not wish to be a trinitarian dogmatist, nor do I assert that a well-developed soul or public has only three moral dimensions. The more I have explored these three, that are enshrined in republican tradition, the more I have discovered them to be empirical realities. But there may be other dimensions that I have overlooked, and possibly new dimensions are being created as our morality becomes more complicated. Such considerations I am content to leave to others. For the present, this trinity, liberty-equality-fraternity, seems to me theoretically sufficient, since the problems of rights, needs, and virtues are still our central problems. Hence, this revolutionary faith of the Enlightenment, so it seems to me, is still tenable and has become genuinely orthodox.

Notes

CHAPTER 1

1. Quoted from Sumner's *The Challenge of Facts,* by Henry Alonzo Myers in his *Are Men Equal?* (New York, 1945), pp. 139–40. Professor Myers gives an excellent account of the divergence of liberty and equality in America, from which I have borrowed extensively.
2. Quoted in Myers, *op. cit.,* p. 122.
3. This is taken from Stalin's attack on Zinoviev.
4. David Thomson, *Equality* (Cambridge, 1949), p. 154.
5. *Ibid.,* p. 153.
6. *Ibid.,* p. 154.

CHAPTER 2

1. Richard Overton, *Remonstrance to Parliament* (1646). Republished in William Haller, *Tracts on Liberty in the Puritan Revolution, 1638–1647* (New York, 1933), Vol. III, p. 367.
2. John Lillburne, *England's Birthright Justified* (1645). Haller, *op. cit.*, Vol. III, p. 269.
3. Haller, *op. cit.*, Vol. III, p. 358.
4. Letter to James Madison, March 15, 1789.
5. The Federalist Papers, No. LXXXIV.
6. *Human Rights*, A symposium edited by UNESCO (1949), p. 268.
7. *Ibid.*, pp. 268–71.
8. Ralph Barton Perry, *The Citizen Decides* (Bloomington, Indiana, 1951), p. 74.

CHAPTER 3

1. Adam Smith, *Lectures on Jurisprudence*, Div. II, secs. 1 and 2.
2. J. Djordjevic, "Le Socialisme et le Droit." Unpublished manuscript. Translation mine.
3. In his *Critique of the Gotha Program*.